PUBLIC RELATIONS
Toolbox

A Collection of Best
Practices for School
Counselors

© 2002
YouthLight, Inc.
Chapin, SC 29036

All rights reserved.
Permission is given for individuals to reproduce materials designated.
Production of these materials for an entire school system is strictly forbidden.

Edited by Barbara Mueller-Ackerman (need cred.)

Editorial Support:
Robert P. Bowman, Ph.D.
Susan C. Bowman, Ed.S., LPC
Renee D. Wildman

Layout and Design by Moon Design

ISBN 2001097912
Library of Congress Number

10 9 8 7 6 5 4 3 2
Printed in the United States of America

PO Box 115, Chapin, SC 29036
Phone: (803) 345-1070 or (800) 209-9774
Fax: (803) 345-0888
E-Mail: YL@sc.rr.com

Dedication

To the memory of Louise B. Forsyth, who taught school counselors and those who work with and train them the importance of public relations in our profession.

Acknowledgments

It would be impossible to produce a volume of this size without the creativity and dedication of many people from the past and present. This is but a small acknowledgement for their very large contributions to this work.

To the ASCA presidents, and their Public Relations and National School Counseling Week chairs in the past decade, whose work and themes are represented within these pages:
1989: Doris Rhea Coy
1990: Beverly J. O'Bryant
1991: Nancy S. Perry
1992: Rosalie Humphrey
1993: Jackie M. Allen
1994: Mary E. Gerhke
1995: Margaret H. Jennings
1996: Carolyn B. Sheldon
1997: Canary C. Hogan
1998   Judith Lee Ladd
1999: Jan Gallagher
2000: Mark Kuranz
1999: Pamela Gabbard

To the Governing Board, under the leadership of Judith Lee Ladd, thank you for "lighting the way" in order to create the opportunity to make this book a reality for the professional school counselors in the field, on behalf of all our students.

Special gratitude to Judy Bowers, the Public Relations Committee and the professional school counselors of the Tucson Unified School System, for the great generosity of their contributions to ASCA in their writings on public relations and parenting, and to Kim Long and the school counselors of Frederick County, Maryland for the contribution of their valuable bookmarks;

To professional school counselors Brenda Melton, Cindy Hamrah Povall, Carol Dahir, Joan Novelli Capaloupo, Jackie Allen, Connie Collins, Lin Avellino and the New Jersey, Pennsylvania, Michigan, Wisconsin, Indiana, Idaho, Texas and South Dakota state school counselor associations for sharing their materials;

To Elizabeth Madden, Tonya Daugherty, Bob and Susan Bowman, and all at Youthlight, Inc. for endless patience, support, forgiveness and mentoring;

To Cheryl Smith and Pat Kochanski and those in NJSCA who recognized my potential and welcomed me as a new counseling colleague;

To friends made at ASCA, particularly Judy Ladd and Dale Robert Reinert, who encouraged and championed my efforts as Public Relations Chair, 1998-2000, and who offered nurturing, friendship and love;

To Blanche Treloar, Sharon Knoller, Marcia Bright, Karen Hagan, Donna Schmitz, Lynne O'Connor, Dennis McCarthy and colleagues and friends in the Springfield, New Jersey Public School System for making even the most difficult work days rewarding and joyous;

To professors Jane Runte and Dr. Betty Caccavo for their mentoring and encouragement as I pursued this wonderful new field and career path;

To Dr. Drew Cangelosi, teacher, mentor and friend, gratitude for challenging me to explore creativity and play and to accept, embrace and master my shadow;

To Dr. Phylis Philipson, who with gentleness and compassion has helped me know grounding and light;

To Jack Canfield and Cheryl Richardson for life lessons in courage and self-care;

To my mother, Rosalind Perlish, whose "big shoes to fill" have challenged me to grow into my own and become all that I can be;

To my beautiful daughters, Jaime and Allison, for their patience and unconditional love while I was growing up;

And finally, to my husband, Michael, for whom I am thankful each and every day; who has held steadfast belief in me and who is anchor, wisdom, model, best friend and, in my life, love personified.

– Barbara Muller-Ackerman

Table of Contents

pub•lic re•la•tions *(pub'lik ri la shens)* **1.** The methods and activities employed by an individual, organization, corporation, or government to promote a favorable relationship with the public. **2.** The degree of success obtained in achieving such a relationship. **3.** The staff employed to promote such a relationship. **4.** The art or science of establishing such a relationship.

— Grolier International Dictionary

SECTION ONE

Building a Frame of Reference

PUBLIC RELATIONS

What is public relations for the school counseling program? For one thing, it is focused. An effective PR strategy contains many of the words and concepts often used when building a school counseling program as a whole. The successful PR program is:

- Planned
- Systematic
- Comprehensive
- Proactive, not reactive
- Collaborative
- Dependent on good communication skills

Before creating and implementing a PR program, school counselors need to spend time determining what they wish to achieve from putting such a strategy into place. This is particularly important because only a continuing commitment to implementing a PR effort will ensure its success.

The PR goals that a school counselor could establish might include:

1. Better visibility for the school counselor and the program.

2. Clearer understanding of the role of the school counselor and program by students, parents, peers and the wider community.

3. Increased ratings on community needs assessment instruments regarding counselor/school counseling programs.

4. Increased confidence and trust in school counselors individually and school counseling as a profession.

5. Enhanced teacher cooperation and support.

6. Increased positive student response to the contributions made by counselors and the school counseling program.

7. Increased awareness among the various constituencies of the school counseling program objectives, accomplishments and services.

8. Delineated outcomes/objectives clients can expect from the counselor and the school counseling program.

9. Increased financial, time and administrative support for existing/new programs.

10. Improved perception of the school counselor as concerned and working with all students.

11. Increased positioning of school counselors as active communicators with clients, students, parents, teachers, administrators and the community.

12. Improved visibility, ensuring that school counselors are considered a vital member of the education team.
13. Improved partnerships, particularly by uniting parents and teachers in meeting the education and counseling needs of all students.
14. Integrated efforts of the home, the school counseling program and the community to improve educational opportunities for all children.

According to the National School Public Relations Association:

"Educational Public Relations is a planned and systematic management function to help improve the programs and services of an educational organization. It relies on a comprehensive two-way communications process involving both internal and external publics, with a goal of stimulating a better understanding of the role, objectives, accomplishments and needs of the organization.

"Educational Public Relations programs assist in interpreting public attitudes, identify and help shape policies and procedures in the public interest and carry on involvement and information activities which earn public understanding and support."

Public relations and your school counseling program

Why should PR be your concern? At its core, PR is the process of driving a concerted communications effort to accomplish one or both of two things: favorable coverage of your efforts or positive influence of an important audience. Used by itself or in combination with other marketing communications (e.g., advertising, direct mail, special promotions or an event), PR delivers a message to the target group, generating recognition and understanding of your program.

By implementing a PR campaign, you commit time and energy to winning the attention of all the audiences whom you wish to reach. The results can be dramatic: heightened visibility, widespread recognition and an increased demand for services.

The critical keys to success, however, are these: commitment, time, creative energy and a focus on the long term. Without these elements, chances of success are proportionately reduced. A PR campaign should not be viewed as a quick fix to overcome a negative perception or a crisis situation. It should instead be a consistent effort built over time.

Achieving results through an effective PR strategy requires the ability to convince your audiences — journalists, parents, other teachers, students and school boards — of the value of school counselors

KEEP IT STRAIGHT

The Top Ten Reasons Your School Counseling Program Is An Excellent Investment

Another way to look at the benefits that school counselors provide is summarized this way:

10. Your school counselor can serve your school as a resident expert on standardized achievement tests, career assessment and planning programs, as well as PSAT, ACT, SAT, ASVAB, and other tests your district might use.
9. Your school counselor can help analyze assessment results and identify strengths and weaknesses, thus helping to give direction to the school's improvement plan.
8. School counselors can help parents and teachers prepare their students for standardized tests and other assessments creating the best assessment conditions at home and at school.
7. School counselors can help students and schools improve attendance, reduce dropout rates, and improve achievement. They can also help students make successful transitions from level to level and from school to work.
6. Counselors can help students develop comprehensive education/career plans through career assessment and classroom guidance activities that target high school completion and exploration of post-secondary opportunities.
5. Counselors can offer professional counseling and guidance, in groups or individually, by certified school counselors who adhere to ethical standards and confidentiality codes.
4. Counselors can help students cope with social problems that affect schools, giving them skills in solving problems without violence.
3. School counselors can lead timely responses when such crises affect our schools, helping students, parents and teachers overcome obstacles when they occur.
2. Counselors can help your schools discover and utilize community resources that enhance and complement the preparation of students for successful achievement of present and future goals.

...AND the number one reason your counseling programs are an excellent investment:

1. Your students deserve the best hope for the future to realize their full potential!

Adapted with permission from the South Dakota School Counselor Association

and the services they offer. It also requires the provision of appropriate materials to support your case and appropriate follow-through to ensure that your message is being treated fairly and with respect.

Taking a realistic approach

Every day, millions of messages bombard us through a multitude of information sources: newspapers, television, magazines, radio and now the Internet. Whether

KEEP IT STRAIGHT

The Role of the Professional School Counselor

The professional school counselor is a certified/licensed educator trained in school counseling. Professional school counselors address the needs of students through the implementation of a comprehensive, standards-based, developmental school counseling program. They are employed in elementary, middle/junior high, and senior high schools, and in post-secondary settings. Their work is differentiated by attention to age-specific developmental stages of student growth and the needs, tasks and student interests related to those stages. School counselors work with all students, including those who are considered at-risk and those with special needs. They are specialists in human behavior and relationships who provide assistance to students through four primary interventions: counseling (individual and group), large group guidance, consultation, and coordination.

COUNSELING is a confidential relationship which the counselor conducts with students individually and in small groups to help them resolve or cope constructively with their problems and developmental concerns.

LARGE GROUP GUIDANCE is a planned, developmental program of guidance activities designed to foster students' academic, career, and personal/social development. It is provided for all students through a collaborative effort by counselors and teachers.

CONSULTATION is a collaborative partnership in which the counselor works with parents, teachers, administrators, school psychologists, social workers, visiting teachers, medical professionals and community health personnel in order to plan and implement strategies to help students be successful in the education system.

COORDINATION is a leadership process in which the counselor helps organize, manage and evaluate the school counseling program. The counselor assists parents in obtaining needed services for their children through a referral and follow-up process and serves as liaison between the school and community agencies so that they may collaborate in efforts to help students.

Professional school counselors are responsible for developing comprehensive school counseling programs that promote and enhance student learning. By providing prevention and intervention services within a comprehensive program, school counselors focus their skills, time and energies on direct services to students, staff, and families. In the delivery of direct services, the American School Counselor Association (ASCA) recommends that professional school counselors spend at least 70% of their time in direct services to students. ASCA considers a realistic counselor-student ratio for effective program delivery to be a maximum of 1:250.

Above all, school counselors are student advocates who work cooperatively with other individuals and organizations to promote the academic, career, and personal/social development of children and youth. School counselors, as members of the educational team, consult and collaborate with teachers, administrators and families to assist students to be successful. They work on behalf of students and their families to ensure that all school programs facilitate the educational process and offer the opportunity for school success for each student. School counselors are an integral part of all school efforts to ensure a safe learning environment and safeguard the human rights of all members of the school community.

Professional school counselors meet the state certification/licensure standards and abide by the laws of the states in which they are employed. To ensure high-quality practice, school counselors are committed to continued professional growth and personal development. They are proactively involved in professional organizations which foster and promote school counseling at the local, state and national levels. They uphold the ethical and professional standards of these associations and promote the development of the school counseling profession.

ASCA Delegate Assembly, June, 1999

the information comes in the form of advertising or as news, it is generated from someone, somewhere. In short, it is a highly competitive environment in which to conduct an effective PR campaign.

That is why it is so important for the school counselor to decide, before creating and implementing a PR strategy, exactly what the goals of the effort will be — and how the results will be measured. Success is more likely when the goals of your PR strategy are limited to two or three. Rather than trying to achieve everything, you will find it more effective to focus on the one or two things that are most important to both you and your audiences.

For example, the challenging issue for you may be to gain the increased support of teachers for your effort and for you to be recognized as an important, contributing member of the education team. This, then, provides the foundation for your PR efforts. You will build and execute a strategy that focuses on this issue. In addition, this goal will guide you to establish your measurement for success: increased support and inclusion on the education team.

Acknowledge that you can't do it all at once, and you're off to a great start!

Becoming proactive

"Top-of-mind" awareness of school counselors should be the over-arching goal of all proactive PR strategies — creating the perception of the school counselor as a dedicated resource, a complete professional and an integral part of any extended school community. Top-of-mind awareness, however, cannot — and will not — be achieved overnight. It is the result of ongoing investments of time, resources and energy, coupled with a commitment to respond at any given time.

No single action or initiative will achieve top-of-mind awareness. But careful strategic planning can build a strong foundation for it. A steady flow of substantive news and insight, promotional activities and other positioning will ensure that, over time, your target audiences think of you early and often.

Is it about me?

One of the hardest challenges to overcome in PR is modesty. Many people would rather turn the attention from themselves and back to the cause or the program. For school counselors, there is no doubt that PR for your program should focus on communicating benefits to others more than selling yourself. At the same time, however, it is important to recognize that you, as a school counselor, are the persona of the program and the benefits that you are endeavoring to communicate.

This means that you must be articulate and passionate about the role of the school counselor in the extended school community. It means that you must be prepared — professionally, emotionally, physically — to take a highly visible role. It means that you need to be creative in the promotional activities you plan and implement — activities that will require 100 percent of your time and energy above and beyond your day-to-day professional duties.

Once you recognize that indeed, it is also about you, then you are better equipped to look at the ongoing benefits of your PR campaign for others in your school community. In planning your public relations program, you need to address the following question:

What are the benefits of a proactive PR effort for the following groups:

- Student Services Personnel
- Students
- Board of Educators
- Parents
- Administrators
- School Counselors
- Community
- Business and Industry
- Teachers

Benefits of school counseling programs

Comprehensive school guidance and counseling programs positively affect students, parents, teachers, administrators, boards and departments of education, school counselors, counselor educators, post-secondary institutions, student services personnel, business and industry, and the community. The benefits to each of these groups include the following:

Benefits for Students

1. Relates educational programs to future success.
2. Facilitates career exploration and development.
3. Develops decision-making and problem-solving skills.
4. Assists in acquiring knowledge of self and others.
5. Enhances personal development.
6. Assists in developing effective interpersonal relationship skills.
7. Broadens knowledge of a changing world.
8. Provides advocacy for students.
9. Encourages facilitative, cooperative peer interactions.
10. Fosters resiliency factors for students.
11. Ensures equitable access to educational opportunities.

Benefits for Parents

1. Provides support for parents in advocating for their child's academic, career, and personal/social development.
2. Develops a system for their child's long-range planning and learning.
3. Increases opportunities for parent/school interaction.
4. Enables parents to access school and community resources.

Benefits for Teachers

1. Provides an interdisciplinary team effort to address student needs and educational goals.
2. Provides skill development for teachers in classroom management, teaching effectiveness and affective education.
3. Provides consultation to assist teachers in their guidance role.

Benefits for Administrators

1. Integrates school counseling with the academic mission of the school.
2. Provides a program structure with specific content.
3. Assists administration to effectively use school counselors to enhance learning and development for all students.
4. Provides a means of evaluating school counseling programs.

Benefits for Boards and Departments of Education

1. Provides a rationale for implementing a comprehensive developmental counseling program.
2. Provides assurance that a quality counseling program is available to all students.
3. Demonstrates the necessity of appropriate levels of funding for implementation.
4. Supports appropriate accreditation and staffing.
5. Provides a basis for determining funding allocations for school counseling programs.
6. Furnishes program information to the community.
7. Gives ongoing information about student competencies and standards for excellence attained through school counseling program efforts.

Benefits for School Counselors

1. Provides a clearly defined role and function.
2. Reduces non-counseling functions.
3. Provides direct service to all students.

4. Provides a tool for program management and accountability.
5. Enhances the role of the school counselor as a student advocate.
6. Ensures involvement in the academic mission of the school.

Benefits for Counselor Educators

1. Enhances collaboration between counselor education programs and public schools.
2. Provides exemplary supervision sites for school counseling internships.
3. Increases opportunities for collaborative research on school counseling program effectiveness.

Benefits for Post-secondary Institutions

1. Enhances articulation and transition of students to post-secondary institutions.
2. Prepares students for advanced educational opportunities.
3. Motivates students to seek a wide range of post-secondary options, including college.

Benefits for Student Services Personnel

1. Provides school psychologists, social workers, and other professional student services personnel with a clear definition of the school counselor's role.
2. Clarifies areas of overlapping responsibilities.
3. Fosters a positive team approach, enhancing cooperative working relationships.

Adapted with permission from: ASCA's "Sharing the Vision, National Standards for School Counseling Programs," Carol Dahir and Chari Campbell.

Note: See the appendix for a reproduceable version.

PROFESSIONAL IMAGE

ike it or not, image is a key element of any effective PR program. After all, it is how something is perceived that will often determine its future success — or lack thereof. Here are some general definitions of image:

- Image is what we think, believe, and feel toward something, even though that image may not match reality.

- Image is the sum of perceptions, attitudes, beliefs, ideas and feelings held about something.
- Image is based on what is seen, felt, touched, heard and believed to be real.
- Image is often developed from personal experiences and observations.

For school counselors, professional image includes the way you look, dress, act, talk and present yourself to others, plus the way you promote your school counseling program. In any PR effort, your professional image will be critical. As you speak to your different target audiences, the media and other decision-makers, always remember that you are the public face of the school counseling program you are representing.

Professional image also includes ensuring that you are abreast of latest developments in the field and in society generally. There is nothing more embarrassing than to be "caught out" on something of which you should be aware.

Past ASCA President Dr. Beverly J. O'Bryant wrote:

"It is our duty (ethically) as professional school counselors to maintain and enhance our 'professional image.' And staying in touch with developing, growing, innovative people in our profession can be fun and very rewarding. It can sometimes be a little disconcerting to learn how little we may know in comparison to some others in our profession, but it can also be very rewarding to learn that we know enough to contribute to the professional growth of others."

Adapted with permission from Wittmer (1993), Managing Your School Counseling Program. Minneapolis, MN: Educational Media Corporation.

What shapes a school counseling program's image?

A public school's image is largely shaped by how that school system appears to the public. The public can observe objective characteristics like the number of luxury cars in the parking lot and then make the conclusion that teachers are overpaid, whether this is logical or not. On the other hand, the image of student services might vary depending on the diverse, subjective experiences of the people who interact with these services.

Attention should be paid to the following factors that can "make or break" a school counseling department's image:

- Any publication you distribute, such as a regular newsletter
- Condition of the physical plant, including the bulletin boards and offices for which you are responsible
- Curriculum design
- Standardized test scores, especially the SAT
- Colleges where seniors are accepted
- Dropout rates/teen pregnancy rates in the school area that you serve
- Student/staff drug and alcohol usage
- Business partnerships
- Student/staff volunteerism
- Teaching and administrative staff outreach and service to community
- Follow-up and feedback delivered in a timely manner
- Adherence to confidentiality

KEEP IT STRAIGHT

Professional school counselors are:

- Graduate-degreed professionals trained in school counseling
- Experienced in dealing with academic and personal issues with students, staff and parents
- Able to suggest options and solutions to problems
- Friends who offer understanding and support
- Helpful and resourceful with information on career choices and post-secondary opportunities
- Good listeners who encourage others
- Responsible and respectful of confidences
- Mediators for students, staff, parents
- Effective communicators
- Professionals who consult with other professionals to better help students and their families
- Knowledgeable about community resources that offer services to meet varying needs
- Visible to students and staff

Professional image is also affected by professional standards. If individual professional standards fall below that of the acceptable median, then any PR effort will need to address this issue quickly — and effectively — before progress can be made in other areas.

The Many Roles of School Counselors

School counselor as human relations specialist

School counselors facilitate systemic change by being a part of and/or leading:

- Community councils
- Cooperative learning groups
- Strategic planning efforts
- Shared decision-making teams
- Advisory committees
- School improvement teams

School counselor as facilitator of team building

Education reform or transformation models such as Total Quality Management (TQM) stress the importance of team building in the early stages of the change process. As trained group facilitators, school counselors are helpful in planning and conducting activities to promote cohesiveness, cooperation and team identity.

School counselor as promoter of positive student outcomes

School counselors are the key players in implementing recommendations from the United States Depart-ment of Labor SCANS (Secretary's Commission on Achieving Necessary Skills) report. This report identifies the following essential skills for successful employment:

- Communication skills
- Interpersonal skills
- Listening skills
- Problem-solving and decision-making skills
- Self-esteem and self-management
- Knowing how to learn

School counselor as resource broker of services

School counselors serve as links to various publics that depend on each other for resources.

- School-based coordinator of integrated counseling services.
- Coordinator of school-to-work transition programs.
- Liaison from the educational system to business and industry.

School counselor as change agent

One of the most important contributions to the success of any change effort is the feeling by all concerned that they truly have been heard and involved in the process. As trained listeners, school counselors are role models, summarizers, recorders, or facilitators of the listening process. In their role as change agents, professional school counselors facilitate change through prevention and intervention for all students. This offers the school counselor an opportunity to be:

- Student Advocate
- Catalyst
- Liaison to Parents
- Systems Thinker
- Provider of Student Services
- Transition Consultant
- Policy-making Facilitator
- Coordinator
- Team Player
- Case Manager
- Leader

This also provides the school counselor the opportunity to position him- or herself wearing different "hats," depending on the PR opportunity that might present itself. For example, there may be a situation in a school community where a strong advocate on behalf of the student body is needed. The situation attracts the attention of the local media and politicians. The student counselor is able to step up to the plate and take on the role of student advocate, highlighting one of the many roles that a school counselor may play.

ADVOCACY

Just what is it that school counselors do? If counselors can't — or won't — explain it, then who will? The following pages include strategies for counselors to use in advocating for their profession and counseling programs. School counseling in the 21st century will occur through the leadership skills and program knowledge advocated by professional school counselors.

Advocacy-focused public relations

Most public relations literature suggests that you phrase messages in positive terms, avoiding negative words and tone. This is good advice: however, when it comes to advocacy for school counseling programs, the message below should rule your behavior:

Never assume that people already understand your program or what you do.

Advocacy is an issue in school counseling because the public at large does not comprehend the range or the value of services provided by school counselors. This provides a great opportunity for school counselors to be their own best advocates by designing quality public relations efforts that inform and enlighten the target groups.

In any strong and effective advocacy-focused public relations campaign, school counselors need to:

Educate…
    the public
Communicate…
    the value of what school counselors do for students
Advocate…
    for the program
and *Be Accountable…*
    for program effectiveness

Adapted with permission from Advocacy Challenge and Opportunity Work-shop, Carol Dahir, Ed.D., ASCA Leadership Development Institute 1998

Organizing your public relations initiative

In putting together your advocacy-focused PR initiative, it is helpful to ask — and answer — the same six basic questions journalists are taught to ask:

Who
Who needs to know? Who makes decisions about your school counseling program? Who seems to be misinterpreting your program? Who is influential in the community? Who are your target groups?

What
What do your target audiences need to know? What don't they need to know? What will help them see the big picture and the important parts, but spare them the details?

How
How do you get the message across? How can you observe the PR campaigns of other organizations and borrow the ideas that seem to work?

When
When is the best time to carry out the PR program? When are good dates and specific occasions that lend themselves to PR?

Where
Where should you focus your attention?

Why
Why is it important to your program and your stakeholders?

The advocacy-focused PR challenge

School counselors are typically trained to advocate for the needs of their students, but not the profession. It is important to advocate in these times of tight

KEEP IT STRAIGHT

Suggestions and Ideas for an Advocacy Presentation

Time allotment
For a presentation to a school board, administrator, or parent group, allow 12-15 minutes (not including questions and answers)

Video
If you chose to use the videos, you won't have to review overheads if there is a need to cut time.

Audio Visual Equipment
If you plan to use overhead transparencies or a PowerPoint presentation, be sure to plan for an overhead projector and screen or a computer projection system. Be prepared to present without overheads or without a PowerPoint display if necessary. See the appendix for sample overheads.

Questions
Practice questions and answers before hand. Prepare for questions pertinent to your public. Prepare for specific situational questions, e.g., "My son had a counselor who told him…" Don't try to answer for someone else's actions. Return the focus to the curriculum role of school counselors.

Participants
Encourage participation and attendance by all counselors in that area, district and school. In choosing who should present, you may want to have a representative from your state school counselors' assocation begin the presentation. However, be sure to include representatives of the local school counselors. Allow the local counselors time to speak to their specific programs in that district.

Practice
Minimize anxiety. Practice the presentation and outline who will say what and when, so everyone understands his or her role. Anticipate questions and practice responses.

Cautionary Note
Be sure you have the involvement and support from the majority of the local school counselors.

budgets when school counselor positions may be under scrutiny by external groups.

Strategies for successful advocacy

School counselors can advocate by:
1. Communicating the purpose of the profession
2. Speaking to the issues of the profession
3. Writing about the issues concerning the profession
4. Acting on important aspects for the profession

Advocacy is a process. Public relations is a product.

Successful steps to advocating for the profession
1. *Analyze the Present Program*
   Is counseling a priority? How are you communicating the counseling program? What resources are available? Who are the people who know your counseling program and are willing to advocate for your program?

KEEP IT STRAIGHT

Positive Recognition Tools

As role models and as change agents, what we do in school has always had an impact on our program's PR, for interpersonal communication is supposed to be our forte. How we choose to use our skills in this area, and the way we view PR, has enormous implications for our effectiveness as advocates.

Some of us advocate for our programs with quiet efficiency. We build our reputations by being effective with the students, by providing quick feedback and follow-up for the teachers and parents and by being resources for our administrators. We earn respect by being respectful and, if we feel great dignity in our work, it may be because we have imparted that sense of dignity through our actions.

Even having accomplished all of that, sometimes — most times — quiet efficiency is not enough.

As our programs are being cut, as our colleagues are losing their positions, as the validity of our work is under scrutiny, it may be time to make a little more noise and garner more visibility for our programs. Does this mean speaking with a loud and militant voice in the process? Not necessarily. We can make noise by being more creative in letting people know that we are there and a valuable part of the program. We can do this through our efforts in the area of PR.

While the obvious interpretation of PR is public relations, Mary Jane Hannaford, who wrote the award-winning manual, "Counselors Under Construction," suggests that another description might be POSITIVE RECOGNITION. The impact that our Positive Recognition can make on the school-wide climate can be enormous and far-reaching. While we as counselors can only go into so many classrooms for so many lessons in a given year, it is the classroom teacher who walks into that room

day in and day out. If their own sense of value and worth is low, it is harder for them to impart esteem and value to their students. If we can build up their sense of being appreciated, then it is not only that professional, but everyone they touch, who has the possibility of feeling valued. We know, without a doubt, that it is easier to give nurturance, easier to impart a sense of healthy self-esteem when you have it to give... and close to impossible when you don't!

2. *Identify the Publics*
   What publics do you need to inform and influence in order to communicate a better understanding and gain support of counseling programs? Have you surveyed these publics? Who are the people within the school system? Who are the people within the community?

3. *Prioritize the Publics*
   Where do you need to start? Who are the contact people? What kind of program do you present to these publics?

4. *Develop a Plan*
   Identify your goals, activities, estimated costs, and completion dates.

5. *Make Commitments*
   Consistency and follow-through supports a strong message.

6. *Evaluate the Plan*
   What is working, what needs to be revised? Have goals and objectives been met? How do

One of the places to find an endless source of Positive Recognition tools is the grocery store. On any day, within the aisles of the market, you can find the shelves loaded with, quite literally, JOY®, CHEER®, HUGS® and KISSES®. Armed with bags full of supplies like those, how much easier it becomes to accomplish our goal.

Many of us read about handing a colleague a roll of lifesavers with a heartfelt message of thanks for what they were able to do for a child. I have heard others talking about using 3 Musketeer's® bars to reflect that partnership between teachers, students and counselors during National School Counseling Week. These small tokens seem to elicit tremendous responses from their recipients. If you haven't tried them yet, when you reach into your "bag of tricks" for some good PR ideas, consider a grocery bag, and try these for any of your client-base. Whether you choose to give them to your colleagues, administrators, parents, or students, the effect is still the same ... wonderful! ... and returns to you many-fold. Ideas are included from a number of aisles but the list is endless, as are both the inspirational messages you can create and the opportunities you have to give them.

Sweetness Abounds in the Candy Aisle
- $100,000® candy bar with the message: You're priceless.
- Milky Way® candy bar with the message: You're out of this world.
- Candy Corn with the message: It may sound a little corny, but I think you're great! Or, It may sound corny, but what you did for that student was terrific.

- Charms® with the message: What you did with that student worked like a charm. Thanks for all your effort on her behalf.
- Chuckles® with the message: What fun it is to come into your classroom. Thanks for sharing your students and their laughter.
- Extra® gum with the message: You're always giving that something extra for your students. Thanks.

Cleaning Supplies Never Seemed So Good
- Spirit® or Tone® soap with the message: What a great sense of spirit you convey to your students. Or What wonderful tone pervades your classroom. It makes my job seem so much easier. Thank you.
- S.O.S.® or Shout® with the message: I know you are going through a difficult time right now. If you need me, just shout.
- Also easy to convey a point with Top Job®, Dynamo®, Fab® and Yes®.

Elsewhere:
- In the cookie aisle are Kudos® for any congratulatory event, Nice biscuits® and Incredibly Great Chocolate Chips®
- You can find Success Rice or Sweet Success protein drink
- Cereals can include Kix®, Total®, or try Lucky Charms® with the message—It wasn't lucky charms, but all your hard work that paid off. Congratulations!

Adapted with permission from NJSCA Counselor, 1995, School Counselor Accountability

you know your activities were effective? Can you support your conclusions with tangible results?

7. *Revise And Revisit Annually*

Advocacy Planning for Individual Programs: Recruiting Advocates

Teachers

Teachers are customers of school counselors. As satisfied customers, they can contribute to the inclusion of developmental school counseling and guidance programs into the school's curriculum and be powerful advocates on behalf of the school counselor.

To ensure that teachers become — and remain — satisfied customers, school counselors can implement the following tactics:

- Develop a written program with goals and objectives incorporating teacher input, e.g., role perceptions, time allocations, development of measurable criteria based on student needs
- Develop communication mechanisms to involve teachers in the developmental program, e.g., school counseling advisory committee; planning developmental units to be taught in classrooms; and ongoing means of assessment and evaluation of school counseling programs
- Develop surveys to determine satisfaction with school counseling and guidance programs along with suggestions for improvement

School Board Members

School board members can be important advocates for school counselors through the adoption and funding of a comprehensive developmental counseling and guidance program, thus ensuring that every child has access to a professional school counselor. Furthermore, school board members can ensure that comprehensive developmental counseling and guidance programs are an integral program component at all levels in current and future educational restructuring efforts.

To elicit and maintain the support of school board members, school counselors can:

- Attend school board meetings on a regular basis and maintain visibility.
- Include school board members on a system-wide guidance committee.
- Support school board members who value school counseling by endorsing their re-election.
- Present programs at school board meetings focusing on counseling outcome data that sup-

port school system goals, e.g., a reduction in the dropout rate, an increase in standardized test scores, and so on.

- Get to know school board members on a personal level.
- Nominate supportive board members for local, state, and national awards.

Administrators

Administrators provide the base of support for school counseling and guidance programs. Through their eyes, they must see the school counselor as a vital ingredient in the organizational and educational success of the school.

- To ensure the continuing support of administrators, school counselors can:
- Provide a clear definition of their role and function.
- Be sensitive to the issues and concerns of administrators.
- Serve as a troubleshooter and problem solver during unexpected times of change.
- Diversify skills to meet projected needs.
- Be accountable with documentation to verify role and validation of need for school counseling.

Parents

Parent involvement is one of the key components of an effective school counseling program. Parents, as advocates, can promote legislation, promote ways to improve counseling and guidance programs and garner wider community support for school counseling.

To bring about strong parental involvement, school counselors can:

- Involve parents in program planning by having parent representation on the counseling and guidance advisory committee.
- Be visible at PTA activities, parent conferences, and other school-related activities.
- Provide workshops on advocacy for parents.
- Keep parents informed by writing newsletter articles about the counseling and guidance program.
- Communicate with parents on current and future needs of students.
- Get parents to contact legislators and share why it is important to have school counseling and guidance programs in the schools.

One of the most effective tactics of an advocacy-focused PR program is to request time to carry out an 'Advocacy Presentation' with one of these important publics.

SECTION TWO
The Stakeholders

REACHING THE COUNSELING PROGRAM STAKEHOLDERS

This section of the book offers PR activities for each stakeholder of your school counseling program. Following each category are reproducible documents that can make implementing some of the suggestions quick and easy.

Over the years we have changed the semantics of a core component in our work. Over time, we have written about and for the school counselors' publics, stakeholders, constituents, customers and clients. However, no matter what we call them, the most important question to ask is,

"Do you know who your publics, stakeholders, constituents, customers, and clients are?"

The answer is that they are the most important persons in the school system. They are the students, the parents, all taxpayers, businesses, seniors, administrators, professional and non-professional staff, the Board of Education, the government, professional associations, the media, bus drivers, child care work-

ers, and any other individual or group who has or may have an impact on our school system. These are our customers.

The customer is not an interruption of our work. He or she is the purpose of our work. We are not doing customers a favor by offering education or school counseling programs as a product for their consumption; they are giving us the opportunity to do so. The customer is not someone to argue with or match wits with. Nobody ever wins an argument with a customer and no one should try to.

A customer is someone who brings us his or her needs and desires. It is our job to care for those needs and desires.

(Adapted with permission of Tucson Unified School District and L.L. Bean by Susan and David Carroll.)

Another way to visualize this is to place yourself in the center with all your publics around you.

"Recognize that you serve many publics. Knowing which publics can assist you, being present where they are, making it known that you are present, contributing a substantive statement whenever appropriate or possible, will go far in having them become advocates for the causes of counseling."

**— Dr. Beverly J. O'Bryant,
Past President of ASCA and ACA**

O'Bryant further suggests that school counselors:

- Identify your publics. Know something about each of your stakeholders' respective needs and agenda items.
- Identify a need of theirs that you can help them accomplish and offer your services.
- Attend receptions, meetings, workshops and parties to which you are invited.
- Keep an extensive guest list of all significant publics, including school and city boards, local and state legislators, CEOs and presidents of significant interest groups who can be invited to all events and programs sponsored by the counselor. That these persons attend is not nearly as significant as them knowing what the school counselor is doing.
- Release Public Service Announcements (PSAs) and press releases before and after each counseling program and event.
- Make a positive impression by articulating needs, facts, statistics, legislation, research and positive information.
- Make follow-up phone calls and appointments.
- Acknowledge, thank and recognize their contributions to you and your school counseling program.

School counselors are accountable to many publics. These publics can be divided into three major groups.

21 Ways to Work With Student Stakeholders

1. Provide incentives, recognition and honor programs for students by working with teachers:
- Send home special letters.
- Make calls home for grade or department improvement, honor roll or overcoming an obstacle.
- Use Certificates of Appreciation, Principal's Awards, Teamwork Certificates for a special act of service signed by the principal, teacher and counselor.
- Implement a "Caught Being Good" recognition program in which weekly announcement are made on the school public address system and you give out reward pencils or stickers.

2. Create a counselors' bulletin board that is attractive, colorful, and in a high-traffic area with a theme that changes monthly and is located where students can get information on careers, self-help and school programs. Bulletin boards and display cases can also be used to highlight new programs, new courses, activities and events of the counseling program as well as volunteer and community service opportunities.

3. Conduct special interest sessions for students. Topics might include:
- stress management
- peer pressure
- test-taking tips
- organization
- job application and interview techniques
- anger control
- maintaining friendships

4. Create and distribute bookmarks with tips on studying techniques, dealing with anger, test-taking, phone numbers of local help lines and agencies serving children.

5. Have a box where students can leave anonymous questions that could be answered in the school newspaper in a "Dear Abby"-type column.

6. Organize and invite students to be on a School Counseling Advisory Board or Students' Guidance Council. Each classroom should be represented. The counselor could meet with the students, get feedback and ideas on the kind of information needed, and utilize students as liaisons to classrooms with counseling and guidance service information.

7. Display posters and signs in prominent areas of the school, depicting interaction between a school counselor and a student. Place signs in classrooms emphasizing the typical pupil need and the appropriate guidance and counseling service. Rotate signs for maximum exposure.

8. Conduct grade-level classroom guidance activities on:
- self-esteem
- safety
- study skills
- school-to-career transition
- conflict resolution
- friendship
- wellness curriculum
- career and college exploration
- ATOD prevention

The first group consists of "clients." The second group is composed of publics within the education system. And the third group includes community-centered groups and organizations.

Each public is unique and will require a specific type of assessment to produce accountability data pertinent to their interest. Accountability instruments must be chosen carefully with consideration for specific counselor publics and with concern for the yield of appropriate accountability data that will demonstrate school counselor effectiveness in terms of student outcomes.

Students want to know how counselors can help them be successful in school and prepare them for

the world of work or higher education. Educators are concerned about high school graduation rates, student behavior, student achievement, student adjustment, and placement data. Community groups are concerned about school-to-work transition and the preparation of students for responsible citizenship. School counselors are accountable to:

Client Publics
- Students
- Parents/Families

Community Publics
- Mental Health Support Services

- transitions
- diversity
- character education
- peer helping in preparation for cross-graded activities and experiences

9. Provide information on how to contact counselors. If you are in multiple buildings, list the days and times when you are available. Have an ad for your services in the school newspaper.

10. Work with all new students to explain the services of the counseling department. Run Newcomers' Clubs or facilitate the training of Orientation Peers who can deliver the same information.

11. Coordinate Advisor/Advisee programs in the school, offering lessons and activities for teachers and students.

12. Facilitate training and retreats, then serve as the advisor for Peer Helping and Peer Mediation programs. Recognize your peer leaders/mediators with certificates, special t-shirts and an end of the year dinner for the work they have done.

13. Have a student serve as school counseling columnist for the school newspaper or enlist a student who is technologically proficient to help design and maintain a counseling department page on the school Web site.

14. Sponsor an art, essay or photo contest on a theme that recognizes humane services or needs. As related contests come over your desk, for example for drug prevention or anti-smoking campaigns, make sure that you distribute

the information to the appropriate staff, such as the art, health or communication arts teacher.

15. Have a week of orientation activities in the fall for each class level. Develop orientation programs at feeder schools each spring.

16. Schedule an annual evaluation of the guidance and counseling services by students. In the elementary schools, needs assessment instruments can be used as both pre-tests and post-tests, helping to give strong feedback on areas where you might concentrate the following year.

17. Become known for helping in non-problem-oriented areas of the school, such as after-school sports and activity programs.

18. At the elementary level, prepare coloring books or puzzles to explain your roles as a school counselor.

19. Set up tables in a common area during lunch with occupational information and other guidance materials. Meet students in places other than your office.

20. Run Career Days or College Fairs. Running Teddy Bear Clinics and Careers on Wheels events in elementary schools are wonderful for student career awareness and raising community support of your program.

21. Make your office a special retreat for students. Magic wands, magnetic sculptures, stress balls, and toys on your desk facilitate putting elementary students at ease. Middle- or high-school art students can create a mural on your walls. Post a message board outside your door.

- Business Partners
- Community Partners
- Community-at-large

Education System Publics
- School Faculty and Staff
- Superintendent
- School Administration
- Central Office, School Board
- Peer Professionals
- Other Pupil Services Personnel

There is a fourth area that school counselors are accountable to: themselves and the school counseling profession.

As school counselors most of us are constantly being reminded that we must be:

Accountable
- To our clients, the students
- To students' parents
- To administration and to the school board
- To the community, business partners and the general public

KEEP IT STRAIGHT

Top 20 PR Delivery Methods

Here is a list of PR delivery methods that are readily available to school counselors:

1. Posters
2. Fliers
3. Awards/Certificates/Recognition
4. Public Service Announcements (PSAs)
5. Bulletin Boards
6. Banners
7. Phone Calls
8. Business Cards
9. Brochures
10. Cable TV presentations
11. Newspaper articles (in school and local community)
12. Videos
13. Parent Workshops
14. Yearly District Calendars
15. Columns in newsletters
16. Bookmarks
17. Grocery bags
18. Placemats
19. Computer (e-mail)
20. Promotional Items (mugs, pencils, buttons, etc.)

Responsible
- For our students' actions, goals, behaviors and competencies
- For counseling programs

Liable
- Under the law
- For our actions in times of crisis
- To ethical practices

ACCOUNTABILITY TO STAKEHOLDERS

Accountability instruments

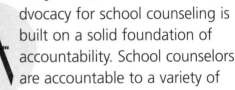

dvocacy for school counseling is built on a solid foundation of accountability. School counselors are accountable to a variety of publics in the school and community. Accountability instruments assist school counselors in measuring their success. Measuring student outcomes is an excellent way of showing the effectiveness of the school counseling program to different groups, such as the local school board, who want to know what school counselors are doing in their programs and what results they're producing.

School boards often question the cost effectiveness of school counseling programs and want to know if a counseling program really makes a measurable difference in student academic performance, school adjustment, readiness to learn, and preparation for the world of work.

Accountability instruments must be chosen carefully with consideration for the type of accountability data that will be produced. School counselors have a variety of choices:
- *Surveys* are data collection tools to solicit answers to questions from participants. A survey can ask questions or take measurements. Surveys may be done with parents, students, school staff, and community members. They may be school-oriented or for the use of the professional association. Surveys are classified by the method of gathering information: personal interview, telephone interview, mail questionnaire, panel, or a combination of methods.

- *Qualitative Questionnaires* are used to measure a participant's opinion after an activity or intervention, such as a series of group counseling sessions. Qualitative research seems to obtain information about the quality of a program or service. Questionnaires vary in length and format and may include open-ended questions.
- *Case Studies* constitute a brief description of a particular counseling case, interventions used, and results obtained. It is important to maintain the confidentiality of student names and particular details that might identify the student. Case studies assist school counselors in improving their counseling techniques, while serving as examples of school counselor effectiveness.
- *Behavioral Observations* are planned in advance and usually refer to behaviors that can be observed and are most likely counted. Informal observations may consist of a running account of what a particular student is doing in a class. Formal behavioral observations may be made by using a checklist and looking for particular behaviors which will qualify a student for a special program.
- *Needs Assessments* are conducted to determine specific needs, in terms of school counseling programs and services.
- *Self-Audits* are specialized needs assessments in which an audit is used as a self-appraisal instrument to determine strengths and weaknesses. ASCA has prepared three self-audits (available at ASCA headquarters) for elementary, middle, and secondary school levels.
- *Experimental (Quantitative) Research Designs* include many variations of pre-test and post-test assessments where a cause or independent variable is present in the study. This type of research is used effectively to measure change as a result of counseling in areas such as classroom behavioral interventions, small group interventions, and individual counseling interventions.
- *Biographical or Portfolio Data* may be collected during an interview, from a written form or from student work samples. School counselors use this type of data to write college and scholarship recommendations.

Practical sources of accountability data

School counselors gather data from many sources to use in evaluating the effectiveness of counseling programs. Accountability data is often used by school counselors on a daily basis. Some practical and accessible sources of accountability data include the following:

- *School Counselor Logs* are used to record data on the amount of time spent in a variety of guidance and counseling activities.
- *School Counselor Record Forms* provide data on types of counseling interventions and referrals.
- *Appointment Sheets* indicate the number of students seen on a daily basis and the length of time for each appointment.
- *Student Profiles* show student progress toward competency, graduation or college requirements, career/life planning and student activities.
- *Student Records* such as transcripts and cumulative folders include grades, test scores, health data, and sometimes teacher reports.
- *Standardized Test Scores* indicate student achievement in relation to local, state, and national norms.
- *Student Assessment Portfolios* provide samples of student work and major projects undertaken for course or graduation requirements.
- *Anecdotal Records* are brief comments on a particular counseling case.

Competencies in Assessment and Evaluation for School Counselors Approved by the American School Counselor Association on September 21, 1998, and by the Association for Assessment in Counseling on September 10, 1998

The purpose of gathering accountability data is to demonstrate the effectiveness of school counseling programs, to demonstrate that school counselors make a difference, and to show through student outcomes that school counseling is an integral component of educational reform and restructuring.

The benefits of accountability are numerous:
- Maintenance of staff
- Additional professional staff
- Improved work conditions
- Expanded budget
- Clerical and/or staff support
- Positive PR
- Expanded services for students
- Peer support
- Administrative and community support
- Business/community alliances
- Increasing awareness of the importance of counseling/counselors
- Increasing parental involvement and support for counseling programs

Accountability is the foundation for successful school counselor advocacy.

When making an advocacy presentation, school counselors must choose appropriate accountability instruments, plan to gather pertinent accountability data, know the interests of the specific public, and carefully select the method of presentation. Accountability assists school-counselors in demonstrating effective school counseling programs.

Have a current vision for school counseling

One of the challenges confronting any PR program is changing a preconceived or ingrained perception. People retain images in their mind that were created from experiences in their own lives, often decades ago. Effective promotion of your school counseling and guidance program involves changing perceptions from what guidance used to be to what it is today. The following approach to school counseling provides a basis of comparison for how programs have changed.

Professional school counselors are:
- Facilitators of change
- Leaders of school improvement
- Partners in educational excellence
- Coordinators of collaborative community efforts
- Managers of student achievement

School counselor's role in educational reform

As previously mentioned, any truly effective PR campaign focuses on one or two goals and uses methods readily at hand to put the strategy into place. One of the common mistakes made during the implementation of a PR campaign is to "over-reach" with

---

KEEP IT STRAIGHT

Top 22 Places to Display Your School Counseling PR Information Material

Here is a list of locations readily available to you for displaying your message and materials:

1. Outside counseling office door
2. Table at orientation program
3. Parent Resource Center
4. Teacher mailboxes
5. Faculty room table or bulletin board
6. Hallway display cases or bulletin boards
7. Copy machine
8. Monthly school newsletter
9. Table in cafeteria for students
10. Board of Education office
11. "Take One" Table outside the Back-to-School Night door
12. Local newspaper
13. Chamber of Commerce
14. Town Hall
15. Public library
16. District or counseling department computer Web site
17. Student handbook
18. Faculty meetings
19. School office counter
20. Booth at a school or community fair
21. District yearly calendar
22. Realtors' offices

Top 20 Public Relations Activities to Coordinate With

There are also many ongoing PR activities that you can link with. Here are some of them:

1. National School Counseling Week (first full week of February)
2. Counseling Awareness Month (April)
3. Timing large-group lessons and school-wide activities into national activities/events/dates already celebrated in school
4. Peer Helping programs
5. Career Days/Career Development Month (November)
6. College Fairs
7. Advisory Committee
8. PTA presentations
9. Parenting Programs
10. Job Shadow Day (falls on Groundhog Day in February)
11. School Board Meeting
12. Human Rights/Diversity Programs
13. "Test Buster"* assemblies
14. Contests
15. Distributing weekly schedule to administrators and Staff
16. Newcomers clubs
17. Staff meeting presentations
18. Staff development programs
19. Health awareness/primary prevention activities (Red Ribbon Week, Kick Butts Day, etc.
20. Family involvement programs

Bowman, (1986). Test Buster Pep Rally.

the tactics used. For example, someone may suggest a press conference to deliver a message when, in fact, a one-on-one conversation with a key journalist might be more appropriate and effective. Someone else may suggest developing an expensive four-color brochure when a simple black and white flier might have a greater impact.

In developing your PR strategy and tactics, consider all the options readily available to you — and then go with the ones that make sense, are easily handled and will achieve your goals.

Visibility is critical

Public relations is all about drawing attention to the message you are promoting. If you fail to gain visibility, then your PR program is effectively dead (unless, of course, you're trying to influence a decision behind the scenes). Scientific studies have shown that something needs to be seen a minimum of eight times before the human brain begins to recognize and absorb the information. In delivering your message, make sure that you are using delivery methods that will be seen frequently by your target audience.

Write to promote

Share with the world who you are, what you know and what you do. Get on your computer and write an article about school counseling and related topics. Then, send it to any of the publishers listed below. Actually, before you send a manuscript, it's best to contact the editors to request a copy of the guidelines for writers, and a sample copy if available. Some of these publishers may pay you for your article while other counselors will thank you for your advocacy for school counselors everywhere.

Check with your local, state and national school counselor and education associations for additional publishers and magazines.

- *Arts & Activities.* Publishers' Development Corp., Dept. WM, 591 Camino de la Reina, Ste. 200, San Diego, CA 92108-3104. Articles on using art for counseling.
- *Class Act.* Class Act, Inc., PO Box 802, Henderson, KY 42420. Articles for English teachers on ways to incorporate counseling activities and language learning.
- *Learning.* Learning, 1607 Battleground Ave., Greensboro, NC 27408. Articles for K-8 teachers.
- *Teaching Tolerance.* The Southern Poverty Law Center, 400 Washington Ave., Montgomery, AL 36104. Articles on how to promote tolerance and understanding between diverse groups of people.

- *Teaching/K-8 The Professional Magazine.* Early Years, Inc., 740 Richards Ave., 7th Floor, Norwalk, CT 06854-2319. Articles for K-8 classroom teachers.

List of Professional Journals

Contact your local library for their mailing or Internet addresses. It is wise to write and request a copy of the guidelines for writers before sending your article.

- *American School Board Journal*
- *Children Today*
- *Educational Leadership*
- *Equity and Excellence in Education*
- *Exceptional Children*
- *Gifted Child Quarterly*
- *High School Journal*
- *High School Magazine*
- *Instructor*
- *Journal of Counseling and Development (American Counseling Association Publication)*
- *Middle School Journal*
- *Native Peoples*
- *Phi Delta Kappa*
- *Principal*
- *Professional School Counseling Journal (American School Counselor Association Publication)*
- *Teacher Magazine*
- *Teaching Exceptional Children*
- *Urban Magazine*
- *Young Children*

Practical proposals for writings by professional counselors

Topics for School Counselor Accountability

1. The effect of school counseling in reducing violence.
2. The effect of the reduction in school counselor/student ratio on the number of at-risk students in a given school.
3. The effect of group counseling on student grades, student attendance, etc.
4. The effect of comprehensive developmental guidance and counseling programs on student success.
5. The effect of career development in elementary and middle-school grades on student motivation and preparation for high school planning.
6. The effect of student placement in college preparation classes in middle school on enrollment in high-school college preparation classes.

7. The effect of individual and or group counseling on class adjustment, readiness for learning, social interactions, etc.

8. The effect of using a particular program or curriculum in the classroom on student success in class, reduction in conflict, attention, critical thinking, readiness for learning, etc.

9. The effect of group counseling on improving student self-concept, attendance and motivation.

10. The effect of individual student contact versus group guidance in preparing students for making academic choices.

11. The effect of a specific classroom guidance unit on reducing stereotyping and prejudice.

12. The effect of using action research in the evaluation of comprehensive developmental guidance and counseling programs.

Prepared by Dr. Jackie Allen, ASCA Past President

PUTTING YOUR PLAN TOGETHER

You've thought about your plan, identified your publics, established some goals for each of these stakeholders for the coming year. The next step involves writing your plan. On the next few pages are examples of plans for the tasks and activities anticipated for a given school year.

The samples are for elementary counselors, but you could construct a calendar or plan that is appropriate for any work setting level. Once you have written down what you hope to accomplish through the year, take time to do the exercise provided through the graph on page 25. By looking at each of the groups to which you outreach, and charting each task under the group and time of year it happens, you will learn a lot about your advocacy efforts.

For one thing, you will see what group you might be leaving out. Or you may notice an imbalance: too much concentrated time with one group to the detriment of the other. For example, you might see that all your parent outreach activities are in the fall and that you don't get back to that constituency until late in the spring. Adding one program for parents in the middle of the year would keep you more visible to that group.

Taking the time to track and evaluate what you are doing gives you a more complete picture of your overall PR campaign and your school counseling program.

While it is impossible to change everything at once, this exercise might point to goals you might set as an individual counselor or a department. Creating a three-year plan, which allows the end picture to be more balanced and effective, could make a big difference in your outreach and ability to make an impact on all the stakeholders you touch.

Planning Your Year*

August/September (Depending upon when your school year begins)
- Establish counselor calendar.
- Establish a Counselor Advisory Committee.
- Assist as necessary with Registration.
- Join school counseling professional associations: ASCA and your state SCA.
- Introduce yourself and your program at the first faculty meeting.
- Develop goals and share with staff.
- Visit classrooms to introduce yourself.
- Meet with each new student and run Newcomers Clubs.
- Begin keeping an accurate, confidential log of all appointments and sessions throughout the year.
- Be on hand to help students find their classrooms the first day.
- Plan to be on the playground before school opens and as bell rings to help with separation anxiety.
- Check with principal on goals for the year.

September/October
- Re-evaluate counselor calendar.
- Complete orientation of new students.
- Plan schedule for parent newsletter.
- Introduce yourself at parent organization.
- Advertise to parenting groups.
- Seek referrals for student groups.
- Begin classroom guidance lessons/presentations and continue throughout the year.

October
- Be involved in Back-to-School Nights/Open houses.
- Begin parent education classes.
- Attend fall professional development conferences if this is when your state SCA holds them.
- Continue/begin group.
- Hold conferences with parents.

November
- Conduct individual parent conferences during P/T conference days.
- Develop classroom guidance lessons.

December
- Develop/improve guidance lessons for 2nd semester.
- Continue to attend school programs.

January
- Plan activities for National School Counseling Week.
- Start planning for grade transitions.

February
- Celebrate National School Counseling Week.
- Attend winter professional development conference (if appropriate).

March
- Conduct or assist with standardized tests (if required).
- Continue parent contact.

April
- Attend American Counseling Association conference (sometimes in March).
- Begin grade transition process.
- Attend IEP Annual Case reviews (if required).

May
- Be willing to participate in formal discussion of student class placements for next year.
- Prepare for closure of groups.
- Notify parents/students of summer school opportunities.

KEEP IT STRAIGHT

Charting PR Outreach by Stakeholder Group

	Client Publics (students and parents)	**Community Publics**	**Education System Publics**
August			
September			
October			
November			
December			
January			
February			
March			
April			
May			
June			
July			

June
- Update records.
- Place logs in a confidential place.
- Consult with staff, conduct needs assessment for next year.
- Evaluate this year and make plans for next year.
- Attend American School Counselor Association annual professional development conference.

*Adapted as a sample, from the Indiana SCA booklet, "Fitting the Pieces Together for Elementary Counselors" 1996.

Practical PR Ideas for Staff Stakeholders

1. Conduct an in-service for the faculty about your school counseling program at the first faculty meeting of the year. After that, consider any of the areas listed under item #10.

2. Reach out to first-year teachers. Present the role of the counselor at new teacher orientation sessions.

3. Explain how to, when to, and why to submit a student referral. Involve them in a discussion and clarify in general terms what help they can expect as a result of a student referral. Invite new teachers to the counseling center/office for an informal, get-acquainted session and show them the resources available for student and teacher use. Share computer programs and how they enhance student learning, achievement and aspirations.

3. Sponsor a counseling department open house for staff.

4. Build staff morale.
- Create a "Wall of Fame" bulletin board to acknowledge accomplishments of building colleagues.
- Create an "Apprecio-gram" bulletin board for thank-you notes and Certificates of Appreciation.
- Provide personal thank you notes recognizing a specific thing the teacher said or did on behalf of you, your program, or students.
- Place small novelties in staff mailboxes throughout the year.
- Buy a box of frozen Swanson breakfast items, called "Great Starts." Take out the food item and tape the box closed. Put it on the front counter in the office, with a balloon floating from it and a morale-boosting message attached about having a "great start to a great new school year." Or save it for a first day of a particularly long testing period. In either case, sign the message card "From your school counselor."
- Try the Counselor Care Kit for a special event like National School Counseling Week or for a first faculty meeting.
- Develop a "Secret Kindness Pal" program among

teachers. Many schools run "Secret Santa" programs but why not include another during National School Counseling Week or the following week during Acts of Kindness Week. On the last day of the program, teachers do not reveal their identities, thereby modeling the lesson that one can give for the joy of it, whether recognized for the giving or not. Thank-you notes still tend to be written, "To the Secret Pal of ..." and then you can post them in the teacher's room around a large sign or poster with an inspirational message about caring, kindness, giving or friendship.

5. Create a resource library in your office, the school media center, or the faculty room that includes information on relevant issues for teachers working with a particular age group.

6. Organize and facilitate a counseling support group for teachers.

7. Initiate and maintain regular articulation meetings with support staff. Custodians, school secretaries, playground aides and bus drivers are powerful allies who often need to be filled in on issues that directly impact our students (such as sexual harassment) but who can be left out of the loop when a child needs TLC due to a family crisis.

8. Team-teach an appropriate guidance lesson on how the subject relates to the future using possible career paths. Provide appropriate follow-up handouts, posters, and discussion questions for the teacher.

9. When teachers go on a field trip, give them a list of questions for students that heighten career awareness, e.g.; if the class went to the market, how many different jobs/occupations did they identify?

10. Provide mini-workshops for teachers, at faculty meetings or staff development days, on topics such as:
- oppositional defiant students
- organizational skills
- ADD kids
- mental health in the classroom
- sexual harassment
- test-taking skills
- integrating career awareness
- crisis management/response
- children of divorce
- children of alcoholics
- teacher-student relationship
- cultural information
- anger management
- decision-making models
- play therapy
- all affirmative action topics
- communication skills
- understanding test scores

11. Act as a resource person for teachers. Distribute information as it relates to curriculum, current events and hot topics, from a counseling perspective; for example, cultural information, bibliotherapy titles for a specific situation in a classroom, school violence, to name a few.

12. Pass on new career bulletins and booklets to teachers and help them relate career opportunities to their subject area.

13. Distribute community speakers resource guide listing speaker names, topic, time available, and so on.

14. Be part of team meetings. Use the opportunity to both present ideas and to elicit referrals. Sitting in on team meetings also makes you an integral part of the team so that classroom lessons are most relevant to what teachers are working on. Providing information about student placement for the next year, adding strategies for challenging situations, and advancing dates and planning for orientations become easy to deliver in this format.

15. Participate in curriculum committees and summer writing teams with teachers on counseling issues. Conflict resolution, multicultural goals, and holocaust education, are all enhanced by a counselor's knowledge and expertise.

16. Give publicity to teachers of student achievements of all kinds.

17. Give immediate feedback to all co-workers. Have feedback forms printed for use throughout the year so that you can leave something for teachers in their mailboxes that day in case you don't have the opportunity to personally sit with them. As an alternate suggestion, have a similar feedback form on your computer so that you can send a quick e-mail.

18. Make the student referral process easy. Have slips available during your first faculty meeting and leave them intermittently in the staff mailboxes. Make sure there is an accessible file in the front office for retrieving more.

19. Develop a guidance and counseling services handbook. Explain counseling from the standpoint of the American School Counseling Association and from the local standpoint. Include objectives and role in relation to other roles, e.g., media, different departments, current thoughts and trends in the school counseling field.

20. Seek out teachers and propose a schedule of when you might be able to go to their classrooms to present large group guidance lessons on the academic, personal/social, and career competencies outlined in the National Standards for School Counseling Programs. Align the counseling curriculum into current lessons that are being taught or into particular challenges a teacher is experiencing with his or her class. In this way both teacher and students are kept informed.

21. Seek leadership roles in local education associations so you can advocate for counselors' positions and point of view. For example, many counselors are on teachers' pay scales and guides but need more than the 10-month contract to coordinate programs and schedules for students before school opens.

22. Survey all staff with a questionnaire designed to determine this year's needs and goals or next year's direction to meet them.

23. Make a list of counseling-related materials available through the library, professional books, in the counseling office. These could include available materials grouped by media, such as videos, CD-ROM, software, books and workbooks. An alternative or additional means of categorizing would be by topic, such as conflict resolution, bullying, self-esteem, careers and test-taking, to name a few.

24. Support a good thing by getting publicity for teachers and their idea, program or event through the media or a bulletin board display. Take pictures and scan them onto the school Web site.

25. Be assertive enough to set limitations on what you do in accordance with this role.

Yearound Morale Boosters for Teachers

1. On the occasion of their birthday, send a card/certificate to each staff member; sing "Happy Birthday" in class.

2. Hang a "Put-Up" poster in the lounge with post-it notes for compliments.

3. Make and distribute a "stress balloon" for each staff member.

4. Give special attention to new teachers.

5. Have interested staff members' select "secret pals" for the year.

6. Offer door prizes at faculty meetings.

7. Distribute clip-and-wear paper "buttons" or signs for various school-related projects/events.

8. Set up a G.R.I.N. Board in the lounge for inspirational posters, sayings, "Take One" pouches of interesting ideas, list monthly staff birthdays and anniversaries guidance referral sheets, and so on.

9. Offer to use the Class Meeting model to help teachers with particular class concerns/problems.

10. Make a supply of "Brag Notes" for staff members to brag on each other. Give a duplicate copy to the principal who collects them and pulls one at each faculty meeting for a special prize.

11. Present a stuffed animal mascot ("Tyler Bear") or facsimile at faculty meetings for certain accomplishments (most parents at conference day, class with the best attendance, etc.) The mascot stays in the teacher's classroom until the next faculty meeting/next accomplishment.

12. Create a "Holiday Stress Reduction Center" in the lounge in December. ("Take care of yourself.") Include holiday potpourri, tapes of holiday music, edible treats, decorations, tips for handling holiday stress

13. "Hats off to a great staff!" Purchase tiny straw hats. Glue small flowers around the brim and glue a pin on the back.

14. Grant wishes for St. Patrick's Day.

15. Plant a silk "Giving Tree" in the lounge on which teachers make positive comments about other staff members

16. In the teacher's bathroom, post a bulletin board with humorous or inspirational thoughts (e.g., "It's a jungle out there!").

17. Make a bulletin board ("Enterprise People Are Unique") featuring a different staff member each week with photos, articles, and a sentence completion sheet of information about the person.

18. Present "K.E.Y." in-services. Offer voluntary monthly programs for staff about particular concerns (e.g., communication, stress, relationships).

19. Have a Year-End luncheon celebration.

Adapted from Ohio School Counselor Association Mentoring Handbook

Practical PR Tips for Faculty and Administrator Stakeholders

1. Provide a faculty resource center where teachers and administrators can come for reading material, relaxation, bio-feedback tapes and other counseling related services.

2. Each day of National School Counseling Week, use a different mailbox stuffer from the list below:

- Piece it together with your school counselor. Include a puzzle piece.
- Rub out those problems permanently with your school counselor. Include an eraser.
- When a Band-Aid® won't hold it together any longer, see your school counselor. Include a Band-Aid®.
- Is your life tied up in knots? Why not unravel yourself with your school counselor? Include a piece of rope.
- For a "quick fix" or a long-term solution, work with your school counselor. Include a piece of candy.
- Chewing on a problem? Why not talk it over with your school counselor? Include a stick of chewing gum.
- Has your cookie crumbled? Talk it over with your school counselor. Include a cookie.

3. Ask a student group advisor to get their group involved in promoting counseling during National School Counseling Week.

4. Use a faculty meeting to highlight your counseling program.

5. Arrange a special meeting such as a breakfast, lunch or happy hour for your faculty so you can socialize and show appreciation for each other.

6. Make an annual presentation to the school board if possible during National School Counseling Week. Be willing to do this any time and often.

7. Have ribbons or buttons made for teachers to wear during National School Counseling Week.

8. Ask your school superintendent to issue a proclamation or commendation letter to all counselors during National School Counseling Week. Publicize it.

9. Be sure to inform all teachers and administrators of your plans for National School Counseling Week well in advance.

10. Hand out cards or information similar to those found in the Appendix on page 47. Or, have these messages printed on the back of your business card.

Practical PR Tips for Parent Stakeholders

1. Create and distribute a flier or brochure describing your school counseling program. Be sure it is placed on "take one" tables at all school events that include parents.

2. Make one positive phone call a day to parents. Calls to students' parents who tend not to be involved

---

KEEP IT STRAIGHT

Counselor Care Kits / Faculty Survival Kits

Each of the items selected for these kits can be slightly different and seems to change from counselor to counselor and state to state, but the gift is always appreciated, whether it goes to school staff during school counseling week or to administrators and school board members. You can lead this activity as a very effective faculty meeting icebreaker at the beginning of the school year.

Materials
- plastic sandwich bag for each "kit"
- Counselor's "I Care" Kit insert printed on colorful paper
- You may include any of the following:
  Tissues
  Emery Board
  Lollipop
  Pin
  Warm Fuzzy
  Penny
  Gum
  Hershey's Hugs®
  Band-aid®
  Rubber Band
  Lifesavers® (roll or singles)
  Paper Clip

Procedures

Place each of the items into a plastic bag with the card below (or some adaptation based on the items you choose to include).

Explanations of items:

Lollipop	To help you lick your problems
Rubber Band	To help you remember to stretch and be flexible during the school year
Penny	To remind you that together we can make "cents" of challenging situations
Paper Clip	To help you to keep things together
Gum	To remind you to stick with it
Hugs	To remind you how much you are appreciated
Tissue	To remind you it's okay to cry
Pin	To help you pinpoint solutions to problems

Counselor's "I Care" Kit

Rubber Band: To remind you of hugging. Hugging makes impossible days better, requires no special equipment, opens doors to feelings, and fills empty spaces in our lives.

Warm Fuzzy: To bring gentle comfort when the world seems cold.

Tissues: To dry the tears of others or to dry our own so we can see the tears of others.

Band-Aid®: To remind you of healing, perhaps hurt feelings of our own or of another.

Lifesaver®: To throw to someone who may need assistance.

Emery Board: To smooth out the rough edges.

Safety Pin: To hold things together.

Bag: All is given in a sandwich bag, for it holds food for thought to be tested and shared with others.

are particularly important. Comment on their child's positive behavior or offer some help.

3. Use Certificate of Appreciation for parent volunteers and PTA Board members. Give them out during National School Counseling Week and during the National Volunteer Week celebration in April.

4. Prepare special pamphlets on topics such as study skills, Parent Teacher conferences, ages and stages of child development, and distribute to parents.

5. Sponsor family/parent workshops, such as family dialogue nights, that foster good communication skills between parents and their children.

6. As schools are looked at more and more to take on community services, consider coordinating a community fair of available resources to parents. Have representatives of mental health agencies, but also driver and voter registration booths, visiting nurse and other healthcare providers.

7. Make known your availability to speak to parent groups. List areas on which you could speak in a brochure. Publish your calendar of dates and topics ahead of time. Topics might include:
- Helping Your Child Succeed in School
- Raising Responsible Children
- Single Parenting Self-esteem
- Living With (and Loving) Your Teenager
- Attention Deficit Disorder
- The Ups and Downs of Adolescence
- Parenting By Heart
- 21st Century Careers
- Being Part of Your Child's Career Search
- Parenting the Strong-Willed Child
- Study Skills for Elementary Children
- How to Talk to Your Children about Tough Topics
- Raising Safe Kids in an Unsafe World

8. Write articles for parents in school and community newspapers; include timely topics and tips for parents. Consider any of the topics that you would speak on, presented in #7, as equally good topics to write about.

9. Prepare a bibliography of child development and parenting books to be distributed at each of your programs and at school event nights. Send one home to parents of students beginning kindergarten. Let parents know where they can be found in the school or community.

10. Invite parents to assembly programs particularly when information is given relative to the testing program, to college admissions, financial aid, orientation programs, course registration.

11. Schedule summertime visitations to school for tours and welcomes to new students and their families so that they are more comfortable with the school.

12. Place an information insert in the report card.

13. Mail a guidance and counseling newsletter home. This can be done as a department with a thematic unit that represents the developmental approach to a given topic. Transitions and Orientation programs across a district make for a great newsletter. It provides parents with information on the program their child is experiencing but also gives them a glimpse into the future, a look at what's coming next.

14. Create programs for dads, for grandparents, for special loved ones.

15. Hold a "tea" and orientation program for new parents, along with some "old" parents, within the first two weeks of when the new family registers a child.

16. Invite parents as career speakers. During Women's History Month, in March, have moms and grandmothers in to present to students. During National Career Development Month in November arrange for parents to be involved in Career programs. Contact parents as potential mentors during Job Shadow Day in February. Have students interview their parents and then have parents in, but have their child talk about what they do; creating a family panel discussion on the occupations at their home.

17. Include parents in those who receive the list of college representatives coming to visit. Have an open invitation to ensure that parents know that the college reps are there for them as well as for their children.

18. Develop a welcome packet for new families. This can include information about the district, your school and/or can be coordinated with community resources as well. Include your counseling brochure and business card inside this packet.

19. Create a page about counseling services and programs in the student handbook and district calendar.

20. If open house traffic won't come to the counseling office, take your program to the main hall. Set up a computer with SAT preparation and career choice software or a CD-ROM for parents to try. Set up a video showing some counseling program that you held such as graduation night, career day, buddy or cross-grade program. Display reference materials and pamphlets you utilize in your counseling program.

21. Develop a brochure for parents about counseling. Let them know what you do and what they can expect from you. Include your mission statement and philosophy. Include a list of the groups you will be running and include a permission form for parents to refer their child. Utilize other school mailings to include this brochure.

committee goes a long way in providing this help. This may help them feel ownership in your program.

24. Incorporate Parent/Family Involvement strategies into your program. They are one of the National Education Goals and the National PTA has created National Standards for Family Involvement Programs. ASCA has dedicated the month of January to focusing on Parent/Family Involvement.

25. One principal has an open invitation for parents to a coffee at the school every three weeks. A counselor always attends. The talk is informal and parents can ask any questions they like and then are given a tour of the building, if interested

26. Offer to be a speaker annually at a PTA/PTSO meeting to inform about developmental needs of children, counselor role, social and emotional needs basic to cognitive learning or any of the other topics listed in item 8.

27. Send a letter to each parent of a senior inviting them to the school. The counselors each take an area of interest and have fifteen-minute sessions with parents shifting at the end of the session.

28. Videotape a parenting course and air it on your local cable channel. That way, parents can still have a chance to "attend" your program.

Strategies to get parents involved
- Parents and community members as guest speakers
- Advisory council
- Panel presentations
- Parents shadow students in school
- Effective parenting presentations
- Family interviews
- Orientation programs
- Workshops on family & home collaborations
- School tours
- Cultural days
- Luncheons
- Breakfasts
- Recognition assemblies
- Career days
- Test-taking/study skills
- Family dialogue nights
- Community mentor programs
- Bibliographies
- Resource center for parents
- Newsletter
- Report-card inserts
- Parent-teacher conference suggestions
- Positive phone calls and letters home
- Parent volunteers
- New family programs
- Hotlines

22. Have an information sheet with addresses and phone numbers and Web sites for adults to find career help. Compile a bibliography of career-related books. Have a similar information sheet for parents seeking help with troubled students.

23. Speak to the PTA about counseling services and programs. Let them know if you have needs for materials or volunteers. While students are helping to orient younger students, entering parents often need orientation by peers as well. Having an orientation

- Provide child care during programs
- Brown-bag lunch or dinner programs

Hot Topics for Counselors to Present
at a Moment's Notice
- Helping Your Child Succeed In School
- The Challenges and Joys of Single Parenting
- Living With (and Loving) Your Teenager
- 21st Century Careers
- Parenting the Strong-Willed Child
- How to Talk to Your Children About Tough Topics
- Raising Safe Kids in an Unsafe World
- Being a Part of Your Child's Career Search
- Parenting by Heart
- Creative Strategies for Living With a Child with Attention Deficit Disorder
- What Kids Need to Succeed at School
- Putting Your Child's Best Foot Forward
- Is Your Child in the Wrong Grade?
- Backpacks on Their Back; Butterflies in Their Stomachs — a parent networking workshop on starting kindergarten
- Academic Success: it's More Than Just Study Skills.
- Hassle-Free Homework
- Parents at Any Age; Grandparents Raising Young Children
- Strengthening Family Bonds Through Family Meetings
- Creating Family Traditions

Practical PR Tips for Community Stakeholders

1. Have a counselor call in on a local TV or radio station.

2. Have local TV and radio stations run counseling public service announcements.

3. Contact local TV talk show hosts and offer to go on TV to discuss counseling concerns on hot topics such as school violence and at-risk youth and to highlight guidance and counseling activities.

4. Contact local newspapers and ask them to do a story on new trends in counseling.

5. Send out Certificates of Appreciation to local groups or individuals.

6. Contact local community and civic groups and tell them you are available to speak about counseling issues (see parent and staff sections for potential topics).

7. Run ads or write articles for local newspapers on your program and any of the topics from item 6. You might want to subscribe to a local newspaper and get to know the editor. Offer to write and submit a week-

ly or monthly column on counseling, parenting and educational issues or ask if they are willing to consider a feature article on special events and activities or on some aspect of your program.

8. Host a thank-you reception for volunteers, especially those who have contributed to your school counseling program.

9. Work with surrounding school districts to sponsor a recognition event to highlight the work of school counselors.

10. Contact the Mayor or Governor's office to sign a proclamation and get pictures for National School Counseling Week. Other themes also warrant counselor-driven effort for proclamations, such as Month of the Young Adolescent, Week of the Young Child, Safe Schools Week, Human Rights Day, among others.

11. In collaboration with community mental health agencies, sponsor an "Agency Fair" to connect school counselors and agency staff.

12. Participate in community drug and alcohol prevention activities, AIDS awareness forums, and pregnancy prevention programs.

13. Have someone calligraph a proclamation promoting school counseling on a large poster. Display it at the courthouse or other prominent community building.

14. Work with the public library staff to create bibliographies of parenting and child development books. If you give out a bibliography in the school, make sure to share a copy with the local public library so they can ensure those books are part of their inventory.

15. Arrange a display about your school's counseling department and, if possible, include a video. Take the display to fairs and shopping malls.

16. Invite community leaders to a school counselor open house and highlight the school counseling program, discussing ways school counselors work with the community.

17. Form an Advisory Council or Committee for your program. Include supportive community members and those who might not otherwise be connected to the school.

18. Arrange for community speakers to present career topics in the classrooms. An easy program to organize is a read-aloud program just after lunchtime. Professionals, from the mayor and other community officials, to different tradespeople, come in, talk briefly about what they do, and read a story to the children. It is often helpful if you select the book to ensure it is developmentally and grade-level appropriate.

19. Start an "Adopt-a-School" program with a community business or industry. Realtors are especially

good businesses to team with as they are always looking for information to better "sell" the school system and, therefore, the homes in their community. Car dealerships are also wonderful partners, offering car simulators for drunk driving awareness programs.

20. Partner with community service clubs. Many are dedicated to specific causes and will gladly supply programs, underwrite peer leadership training, and many have ample handouts to share with the schools in support of their cause.

21. Organize community service projects in which students can participate. Many states are now making this a graduation requirement, so your relationship and outreach to the community on behalf of these students is critical.

22. Begin a mentoring program pairing at-risk students with adult mentors.

23. Plan a Job Shadow Day in the community; arrange for students to visit businesses and government agencies.

24. Inform the general public about the services a counselor offers. Have children help you develop the

exhibit. Place it in the public library during National School Counseling Week.

25. Coordinate a Career Awareness Day. Community resource persons and members of the military can be invited. Allow students to attend during designated periods. Keep groups informal; allow students to get answers to their questions regarding the different occupations.

26. When appropriate, make use of news releases to newspapers and radio stations. Don't wait for someone else to take the initiative. Know the policies of your school system; if press releases must be produced by a public relations person, supply them with the facts. Otherwise, write your own releases keeping in mind the basic requirements of a good news article.

27. Accompany students who receive scholarship awards given by community service organizations.

28. Make club sponsors aware that you are willing to help contact resource persons to speak to their group.

29. Contact the chairpersons of your local service organizations and arrange to be a speaker at one of the meetings. Discuss the importance of occupational information. Explain how important it is for students to be able to talk in an informal atmosphere with someone who is actually working at a particular job. Provide them with a guide for their talk. Have each member who volunteers to talk to students complete a Career Speaker Reference Card. Be prepared to give each volunteer the names of students who are interested in the job or jobs he or she is qualified to speak on. Discuss the kinds of jobs students at various grade levels would be interested in and the significance of the changes they make as they progress through school. Relate this to the need for career guidance and counseling.

30. At the end of the year, whether you have had a Career Day, a job shadow program, a read-aloud program, or a mentoring program, be sure to recognize all volunteers from the community for their efforts. Present an award at a thank-you luncheon.

SECTION THREE
National School Counseling Week

The celebration of National School Counseling Week, the first full week of February each year, affords school counselors a not-to-be-missed opportunity to share their visions with their stakeholders. It is a time to visibly highlight ongoing efforts as well as a time to celebrate the unique contributions that school counselors make to the school setting. It is an ideal week to raise awareness about the level of professionalism that we bring to our work all year long.

If any of your stakeholders are unaware of the content of the National Standards for School Counseling Programs, of the components of a comprehensive developmental model, of the Ethical Standards which govern the school counseling profession, or, fundamentally, if they are unclear about the very role of the school counselor, then this is the perfect week to educate them.

The American School Counselor Association, the national organization that represents the profession of school counseling, incorporates within its identity, mission statement and strategic planning framework, all the tools, strategies, and support to ensure excellence within the field. Avail yourself of ASCA's many resources to help you plan this most important week in our calendar.

No matter what time of year you read this, celebrating National School Counseling Week, the first week of February, may not have even made the already long to-do list you are working on in order to complete this month. When you are prioritizing the many things you are doing — events, activities, programs, lessons, sessions, workshops, applications, accountability logs, consultations, calls to parents, peer training, and referrals — please consider adding to those priorities getting ready for a week that offers you a chance to make that long list public. National School Counseling Week gives you a not-to-be-missed opportunity to showcase all that you do on behalf of our nation's children in your role as a professional school counselor.

Planning for National School Counseling Week: Seven items you will need for your celebration!

1. Countdown Calendar

A countdown calendar is provided as you work through which activities and which stakeholders will be included in your festivities. This stands as only a suggested list of how to plan for the first week in February.

2. Audio and Video Spots

ASCA, along with many state school counseling associations, has developed PSAs to publicize and promote the profession of school counseling. Call ASCA and your state SCA to find out what is available to you. Or, in advance of the week, have a student from the high school shadow you and help you create your own video. Then, contact radio and cable TV stations and ask them to air these spots during National School Counseling Week.

3. Public Service Announcements for use in school

Many samples of PSAs are provided in the appendix. Whether they are read by students over the public address system in school, or used in daily bulletins, they should give you many ideas for creating your own.

4. The Certificate of Appreciation

A certificate of appreciation can be used during National School Counseling Week to give special reecognition to those who've helped you in promoting your school counseling program.

5. The Proclamation

From year to year, proclamations have not changed much in terms of text. We have provided a representative sample in the appendix for you to customize. Bring it to your mayor, superintendent, principal or other town or school dignitary for their signature.

6. The Press Release

Guidelines are provided on how to write a news release and a sample copy of what has been used in the past is included in the appendix. The most effective use of the press release is to add a number of paragraphs on what your school and counseling department are planning as celebration week activities. A calendar of events is a good thing to include in the counseling column of your school newsletter. Include dates, times and locations of events so that all stakeholders can easily see what is being planned for them.

7. Technology

The computer is a highly effective way for us to communicate with each other and with our stakeholders. Bringing it closer to home, if your counseling department is on your school Web site, be sure to add the press release and your calendar of activities to publicize the week.

National School Counseling Week
preparation begins early!

To effectively reach each of our stakeholders, advance planning is a must. Creating an action plan to coordinate those efforts and dates on the calendar means using your calendar in the late fall and early winter to ensure a smooth week in February. Possibilities abound.

Legislators/Dignitaries

While ASCA works to achieve national recognition and your state school counselor association works with your state governor's office, individual school counselors and school counseling departments can contact their local mayors and superintendents of schools offices to have a proclamation signed. Getting dates, and arranging for a photo with local press requires finding out the time your dignitaries need and your newspaper requires.

School Board

The agenda for school board meetings fill quickly. There are traditionally two meetings a month and only one is considered an open, or public, session. If you and your counseling colleagues are going to make a presentation on your school counseling program, calling the board of education secretary now for a time slot is essential.

Parents

Planning a workshop, open house, or "parenting fair" to coordinate with National School Counseling Week is a natural. Making it happen - finding a date with your principal, making sure that it is publicized in January's school newsletter, gathering your handouts and including the date on your calendar of National School Counseling Week events - requires advance preparation.

The role of the school counselor and the Ethical Standards for School Counselors are available from ASCA. Other important handouts are contained within the "Standards for National School Counseling Programs" document and its companion edition, "Vision into Action: Implementing the Standards."

These handouts are equally important in clarifying your role to faculty, administrators and school boards.

Business Leaders

Include your community leaders in your National School Counseling Week outreach. Ask to be on the agenda at a chamber of commerce program or at your local Rotary Club. The speakers for these programs normally present only 15-20 minutes before or after a meal but it is a wonderful opportunity to showcase your program. One effective way to do this is to have students come with you to talk about peer programs or mentoring programs you have coordinated which have community impact. An open house at your school or mentors breakfast, with business people and their mentees, could be scheduled as an alternate idea for focusing on this segment of our stakeholders.

The Community and the Media

Consider asking a high school communications team if they can arrange to shadow you while you are going through National School Counseling Week events. By taping the programs and lessons you are doing this year, you will have a video you can use in later workshops, school board presentations, and for airing in April during Counseling Awareness Month.

Making calls now for deadlines of local newspapers also ensures that your news release of the calendar of the week's events comes out in advance, the last week of January, rather than half-way through your celebration week.

Faculty and Administrators

Getting on the agenda for the faculty meeting falling in the first week of February requires advance consultation with your principal. Putting out invitations for thank-you breakfasts or lunches requires lead time as well. Deciding what your outreach to staff will be, from counselor care kits to certificates of appreciation, from a snack at the faculty meeting to a basket of goodies on the sign-in counter, from handouts in the mailboxes to personal notes of acknowledgment, all demand that you sit and itemize what you need and how long you will need for it.

Students

Scheduling developmental guidance lessons during National School Counseling Week requires advance sign-up time. Poster or essay contests can be run during the week with winners announced at a culminating assembly program.

When you looking back at the list of our stakeholders, you may be overwhelmed by the depth and breadth of the suggestions and potential outreach to be realized. To overwhelm is not our intent. If you are within a very large counseling department, with many counselors to split the load, then perhaps the comprehensive outreach is doable. If you are a lone practitioner on multiple campuses, the list becomes almost inhumane for one week and is better spread out over your year. The point is not to do it all, but to do something, to start somewhere. You do so many incredible things in the course of your year on behalf of our students. This is the week to share the information about the resource that you are. Whether you

start big or small, just start! Let your stakeholders know the beacon that you are. This is the week to highlight your programs. This is your week to shine!

PROMOTIONAL MEANS

Writing

Publications offer an excellent resource for school counselors to promote their profession and program. Begin with your school community, and highlight guidance activities in your school. Ask the PTA to include a counselor's corner in its newsletter. The message is that school counseling programs are beneficial.

A timely article to the local newspaper on school safety in the school district and how school counselors are helping students deal with conflict is likely to be published. Contact the education reporter and let him or her know of a special event, a program or service you are providing. Have several counselors write about successful guidance activities at their schools. Submit them to the local newspaper prior to National School Counseling Week.

Spotlight an outstanding school counselor who has been a leader, who has created an innovative program or has had a distinguished career. Describe the counselor, the programs, career highlights and involvement in professional associations.

Write an article about a guidance program that has been successful in the district, such as career development, dropout prevention/intervention or conflict resolution. Get a parent to write a letter to the editor about how the school counselor helped his/her child. Review the publishing guidelines for a professional journal and submit an article.

PSAs For Radio and Television

Public Service Announcements can be used to inform the community about an event or idea that may help to publicize your counseling program. A PSA is generally between ten to sixty seconds in length. Many PSAs are aired each day by commercial stations. Contact the public service director at the station, and follow the guidelines below to get your PSA on the air.

- Develop copy that is basic and to the point. It should by typed in capitals and double-spaced.

- Include your name, address, and phone number; identify yourself as the contact person.
- Give the name of your organization.
- Indicate whether you are enclosing a slide and/or tape.
- Mail the copy three weeks in advance unless station policy differs.
- Designate the PSA start and stop dates.

See the appendix for sample PSA scripts.

News Release Guidelines

Counselors need to publicize the programs and services they provide for their populations to be successful advocates for their profession. Simply follow the guidelines listed here:

1. Contact and compile a media listing. The list could include key people to whom you will be sending the information.

2. Call, introduce yourself and establish rapport with the person. Find out the best time to call and how much advance time is needed for the information to be scheduled for airing or printing. Inquire about their preferred writing format for providing information.

3. Include in the news release your name, office and home phone numbers (always list two phone numbers).

4. Use your letterhead stationery. Always open the letter with an "Attention To: Person's Name" to ensure your letter reaches your contact person and the correct department. On the envelope, be sure to "route" your letter, with an "Attention To: Person's Name" on the envelope. Remember, whoever reads your letter will be in a hurry and must be able to see at a glance the focus and content of the article

5. Use a standard journalistic format, keeping the article double-spaced on 8-1/2 x 11-inch standard paper. Limit the article in length. Right and left margins should be 1-1/2 inches.

KEEP IT STRAIGHT

Countdown Calendar for National School Counseling Week

With four or more weeks to go:
- Meet with your department and plan theme and delegate tasks and activities.
- Ask for time on your school board's agenda.
- Contact the mayor, governor, and/or superintendent (depending on the scope of what you are planning) to arrange for proclamation signing and date for photo session.
- Order giveaways for staff, administrators, school board, student.
- Clear dates with principal for open house, parenting program, assembly, faculty meeting slot.
- Plan open house, parenting program, or other outreach to this stakeholder.
- Check ASCA Web site, *www.schoolcounselor.org*, for ideas.

With three weeks to go:
- Generate calendar of events to include in the February school newsletter.
- Select handouts and brochures to distribute during the week.
- Contact high school audio-visual department to arrange for taping of events, lessons, and activities.
- Prepare faculty meeting presentation and parenting/PTA workshop.

- Generate list of who will be receiving certificates and prepare mailing labels.

With two weeks to go:
- Send a press release about National School Counseling Week to your local newspaper.
- Arrange for a photographer to be at the proclamation signing.
- Send invitations to open house.
- Select students to read PSAs during the week.
- Publicize poster and essay contest.
- Run off handouts and brochures for the week.

With one week to go:
- Put certificates of appreciation in mailing envelopes.
- Finalize school board presentation; order overhead or projection equipment for PowerPoint presentation.
- Send home reminder for open house.
- Put sign up sheet in office for class lessons.
- Have students practice PSA reading; arrange memo to teachers for students' release.
- Put breakfast invitation on school office counter for staff.
- Create bulletin board on school counseling.

6. The article should:
   a) Follow the "five W's" as outlined in the inverted publicity pyramid (see diagram).
   b) Use concise concepts and language. Avoid technical jargon and terminology. Keep sentences and paragraphs short. Paragraphs should be not more than three lines.
   c) Put the main facts first and the smaller details last. The editor will adjust the length according to the space available.
   d) Write the article in the third person. Stick to the facts, offering no opinions unless quoting someone else.

Possible Activities

Activities for National School Counseling Week Past Successes! Future Triumphs!

This is a time for grass-roots celebration. From individual counselors in single schools to counseling departments within a district, to state school counseling associations, to ASCA, activities are planned to celebrate our profession. As you are planning your week for this year's February celebration, it may be helpful for you to take a look at what counselors have done across the country in prior years. These suggestions, reported by state presidents-elect as well as individual members, come from past spring issues of *The ASCA Counselor*. In keeping with the concept

KEEP IT STRAIGHT

The Inverted Publicity Pyramid

Who?
What?
Where?
When?
Why?
How?
Important Details
Miscellaneous Information

of outreach to each stakeholder, the suggestions are listed by group. As you fill in your National School Counseling Week planning form, be sure to include one item for each stakeholder group.

Teachers
- Provide pencils with counselor logo, snacks for the faculty and staff and promote "School to Work" Week.
- Share special inspirations each day over intercom or in teachers' mailboxes.
- Put ideas for stress relievers on bookmarks for teachers.
- Give a packet of hot chocolate and a note to "take a break on us" from school counselors.
- Distribute a small coupon book to all faculty redeemable for various "time" items (covering a class, a small talk, etc.).
- Make popcorn and soda available for teachers during their planning period.

Schoolwide & Multi-Group
- Announce National School Counseling Week on a marquee in front of the school building.
- Distribute a brochure describing the role of the school counselor.
- Construct bulletin boards to celebrate the week.
- Decorate the halls with "What is a School Counselor?" mini-posters.
- Promote career exploration. Each day include a different activity, such as guest speakers in the classroom, booths in the gym as a career fair, career-cluster dress-up day, business/college T-shirt day.
- Organize a reception for staff, business leaders and students with the purpose of educating individuals about professional school counseling.
- Provide a breakfast to honor and educate counselors and administrators. For example, in Pima County School Districts, Ariz., 350 counselors and administrators from seven school districts enjoyed breakfast and a speaker to honor counselors. After the breakfast, 20 non-profit agencies provided an agency information fair.
- Provide snacks for teachers and administrators while presenting workshops on the school counseling program
- Distribute "3 Musketeer's®" candy with a slogan urging that counselors, teachers and administrators work together sharing a vision for all students (adapted to lighting the way for all students for a different theme).
- Provide doughnuts and coffee in the career center/counseling office.

- Name school counselors "person of the day" in each building for each day of the week.
- Name an alternate "person of the day" to give recognition to someone in your building who advocates for kids.

Students
- Have second graders illustrate how school counselors have helped them.
- Conduct classroom guidance lessons during the week.
- Have students present notes, letters and videotaped expressions of appreciation to counselors.
- Host a Student Appreciation Day.
- Encourage students to perform public service announcements on a counseling-related theme.
- Appear on an educational or cable channel to promote career development for students.

Business & Community
- Invite local newspaper to interview counselors.
- Schedule a video on school counseling to be shown on local cable network.
- Host receptions and ask the newspaper to print articles on tips for parents, written by counselors.
- Work with your Governor to issue a proclamation.
- Send news releases to all newspapers in the state.

State SCA Ideas
- The state association president in Connecticut was interviewed by a popular radio station and the state association newsletter featured a page on how to advocate for the profession.
- Special license plates were made available through the states of Illinois and Indiana.

Administrators and School Board
- Have the school board issue a proclamation honoring the accomplishments of school counselors.
- Provide a "Counselor Care Kit" kit to the administration to recognize counselors.
- Do a slide/PowerPoint presentation to the board of education on the role of the school counselor.
- Give a gift to each school board member.

Parents
- Schedule parent advisory council meetings to coincide with the week.
- Host a Parent Appreciation Day.
- Write a note of appreciation to each faculty member. Honor professional school counselors in your school newsletter.
- Invite parents to attend large group (classroom) guidance lessons and followed up with handouts to extend the lesson taught at home.
- Invite parents to attend a regional conference during National School Counseling Week.

- Have counselors receive a congratulatory memo from the superintendent, thanking them for all their work in this important role.
- Make radio announcements for parents on a local radio station.
- Attend breakfast hosted by community supporters to honor counselors.
- Promote the week through peer helpers by putting their pictures in the local newspaper.
- Attend state school counselor associations offering free workshops to counselors underwritten by sponsorships.

Other Suggested Activities
- Bring a proclamation to your local superintendent or mayor for signing.
- Have students deliver PSAs each morning — perhaps a biography of a different school counselor daily, or highlights of counseling-based programs and services.
- Put inspirational readings at the copy machine for people to read while they are waiting. These are also wonderful in the faculty room or on the mirror in the teacher's lounge.
- Create a calendar where you plan an activity for a different stakeholder each day; handouts at an open house for parents, classroom lessons or a special poster contest for students, thank-you brunch and handouts for staff, school board presentation, articles in the local paper (use press release included in this section) for community outreach. When you send your certificates of appreciation to board members and administrators, be sure to include the calendar of celebratory events.
- Create a counseling department link for your school's home page. Launch its debut during National School Counseling Week.

Posters/Bulletin Boards/Quick Gifts
Using available items, get students to create some of the following poster or bulletin boards. In addition to the theme, posters should also list what counseling services are offered or use the "catch phrase" on cards and attach them to the item indicated.
- A small hand mirror, with a drawing or magazine picture of a student: "School counselors help us see the positive side."

- Several mirrors: "Counseling helps you… reflect on life skills." Each mirror would have a life skill, such as understanding your strengths and weaknesses, making better decisions; acquiring better study habits; developing better leadership skills; and identifying your abilities, interests and aptitudes.
- Several erasers: "School counselor help us erase our mistakes. Oops." (variation: "our worries")
- On black posterboard, use white posterboard in the shape of a light bulb: "Counselors light the way." (variation: "help us plan a bright future")
- Several light bulbs: "Seeing your counselor for help is a bright idea." Each light bulb has a question or statement: "Do you have a problem?" "Need help with your future?" "Counselors care about you." "Counselors welcome parents."
- A ruler: "Counselors help us measure up."
- A CD: "Need someone to listen? See your school counselor."
- Glue stick: "Counselors help us out of sticky situations."
- Glove or outline of hand: "Counselors lend us a helping hand."
- Band-Aids®/medical supplies: "Counselors help heal our hurts."
- Sewing kit: "Counselors mend hearts."
- Picture of a telephone: "Need someone to call on? Talk to your counselor today."
- Use popsicle sticks to make miniature hurdles: "Counseling helps you over the hurdles." The hurdles may include: study skills, self-awareness, personal problems, career choices, understanding graduation requirements and future plans.
- Cheerleader pom-poms: "Here are some counseling services to cheer about." Services may include: career development, consulting, group guidance, individual counseling, coordinating, and assessment.
- Umbrella: "Find shelter under the school counseling umbrella." On the umbrella, add the following: counseling, information, developmental guidance, educational planning, and careers.

Thanks to Brenda Melton, ASCA PR Chair 2000-2001.

Appendix

PRACTICAL EXAMPLES OF MATERIALS TO USE WITH STAKEHOLDER GROUPS

NATIONAL SCHOOL COUNSELING WEEK

Practical Examples of Materials to Use with Stakeholder Groups: Students

Some bookmarks to share with your students

LET'S TALK ABOUT...

Peer Pressure — Part 1

Kids hear the phrase "peer pressure" all the time. What does it mean? It means having peers (people your own age) trying to influence how you think or feel. It can be positive, as in being encouraged to join the band or go out for baseball. It can be negative if you are being influenced to use alcohol or drugs, to shoplift or to skip school. How do you decide?

Know who you are and what values are important to you. Don't be afraid to make your own decisions. Think before you act. Consider how you will feel about your decision later. How will the people who care about you feel? Whatever you decide, you must be willing to accept the consequences. If you are going against negative peer pressure, look and act confident, even if you feel nervous. You can say, "No, thanks. Let's do something else instead" and have some ideas. Or simply say, "I've decided not to do that anymore." When you say no, congratulate yourself. If you fail this time, please, try again. Good luck.

This message has been brought to you by your school counselor. Contact the counselor in your school for additional information.

LET'S TALK ABOUT...

Peer Pressure — Part 2

When your peers, people about your own age, try to influence how you think or act, you are experiencing peer pressure. During your middle and high school years, you'll make many important decisions. Peer pressure can make these decisions difficult.

One key to handling peer pressure is to learn to be your own best friend. When you feel good about yourself, handling peer pressure is a lot easier. You make your own decisions because you know what is right for you. When you know what's important to you and the values you believe in, you will be able to handle peer pressure.

In every decision you make you should find out what's really going on and then think about the consequences of your actions. Ask yourself…Will I feel good about my decision? Will people who care about me be disappointed in my decision? Then decide what is right for you. Whatever you decide, you must be willing to face up to all the possible consequences.

It is important for you to make your own decisions. Know your values and act on them. Take the time to make a good decision, considering all the consequences. Know how to resist peer pressure. Don't let your peers decide for you!

This message has been brought to you by your school counselor. Contact the counselor in your school for additional information.

LET'S TALK ABOUT...

If You Think You Can't Go To College Or Are Worried About Preparation For A Career

Think you can't go to college? Sure, colleges have high standards for admission that usually include a record of good grades, a strong academic program, teacher recommendations, involvement in leadership or extracurricular activities, and satisfactory scores on college admissions tests such as the S.A.T.

A goal of our school is to empower all students with the skills necessary to continue and succeed in college or in a specific vocational field if they so choose. Your school counselor is available to assist you as you plan an academic program to prepare for your future. For students who might not meet the high standards required for admission to a four-year college, your counselor can help you explore junior and community college opportunities that offer other routes to a college degree. Your school counselor can also direct you to opportunities in a career, trade schools, or apprenticeships where you can continue your education and training for a career after high school graduation.

This message has been brought to you by your school counselor. Contact the counselor in your school for additional information.

*Some bookmarks to share
with your students*

Conflict Resolution

There are ways to settle conflicts peacefully without fighting, without running away and without going against your feelings or beliefs.

Resolving conflicts peacefully helps you to stay safe, feel good about yourself, and learn to respect others.

Some of the ways that conflicts can be settled peacefully are: first, calm down and decide if there really is a problem. Think of solutions, weigh the results, and choose a plan.

When settling the problem, be a good listener. Avoid interruptions and ask questions after the other person has presented his or her side. Repeat what you have heard to make sure you understand what the problem seems to be. Present your side of the conflict. Then negotiate a solution. It is sometimes very helpful to have a third person who can be impartial to help brainstorm ideas and develop solutions. This is where your school counselor can help.

This message has been brought to you by your school counselor. Contact the counselor in your school for additional information.

Anger

As humans, we all feel angry during many day-to-day situations. Anger is a normal, healthy feeling to experience, although it can be a strong, even uncomfortable emotion. Children and adults are learning that anger is OK, and that they can learn to deal with this emotion in constructive and positive ways.

The first step is to acknowledge that you're feeling angry.

Step two: relax and cool off.

Step three: think of all the choices you have to cope with your anger.

Step four: do something that won't harm you or anyone else and will still express your anger, such as writing your thoughts down or stating your thoughts and feelings assertively but not angrily to the appropriate person.

Work on learning the signs that announce the onset of anger. These may be tightening of the muscles or messages to oneself.

This message has been brought to you by your school counselor. Contact the counselor in your school for additional information.

Preparing for the SAT / ACT

While scores from tests such as the S.A.T. or the A.C.T. are required and used by virtually all college admissions offices, they are by no means the only factors considered. Good grades, a strong academic program, and involvement in leadership or extracurricular activities are also important.

However, there are some things you can do to help prepare for the SAT or ACT First, there is no substitute for taking challenging courses. Algebra and geometry are essential math courses. Second, the more time students spend on independent reading, the more easily they can develop a strong vocabulary that will improve their chances on the verbal section. Students should also become familiar with the format of test items and practice working with the time limits for each section on the sample test.

For additional preparation, you might consider a preparation course that will instruct you on helpful test-taking strategies over the course of several weeks. For more information about preparing for these tests contact your school counselor.

This message has been brought to you by your school counselor. Contact the counselor in your school for additional information.

*Some bookmarks to share
with your students*

Selecting and Applying to College

Are you wondering where to begin? Do you feel overwhelmed with all the choices available? There is no doubt the process can be confusing, but we can help you by breaking this big job into manageable steps.

First, during your sophomore and junior years, begin the college entrance-testing program. This includes taking the PSAT (Preliminary Scholastic Aptitude Test) in your sophomore year for practice and in your junior year to qualify for the National Merit Scholarship. Then take the SAT I (Scholastic Aptitude Test) and ACT (American College Testing program) during the spring of your junior year and possibly the fall of your senior year.

Next, visit your school's guidance office to discover the many resources available, including the college and career searches that are available free of charge.

Also, make appointments to meet with college representatives when they visit your school.

Even more importantly, make plans to attend college fairs as well as visit and tour campuses that interest you. Finally, don't hesitate to visit your school counselor to become familiar with the application process.

This message has been brought to you by your school counselor. Contact the counselor in your school for additional information.

Decision-Making

You just received a call from your best friend, Jamie. Jamie's birthday is Saturday and he/she has tickets to the Orioles' game. The Orioles have been your favorite team for a long time and this year they are now number one. You are thrilled at the idea of going to the game. But you remember a prior commitment to your parents on Saturday involving work around the house. You promised you would have the list of chores done by five o'clock. Jamie wants to leave at twelve. Today is Wednesday. How can you solve this problem?

Decision-making skills are often helpful in situations like this. The first step is to identify the problem. In this case the problem is a conflict in time involving a commitment to parents and an invitation from a friend. Next list three possible solutions to the problem.

Here, the three solutions might be: 1) Tell Jamie you have made a prior commitment and cannot go; 2) ask your parents if they could do the chores so you can go with Jamie to the game or 3) reschedule your time so you can complete the chores by twelve on Saturday.

Then check out the advantages and disadvantages of each solution. For example, if you choose number 1, the advantage would be you would not let your parents down, but the disadvantage would be you would miss the game. Finally, choose a solution and determine how you will know if you are successful in the results. If you should choose number one, you will know you are successful if you satisfactorily complete each chore on the list.

Again, the steps are to identify the problem, determine three solutions, examine the solutions for advantages and disadvantages, choose a solution, and determine your measure for success.

This message has been brought to you by your school counselor. Contact the counselor in your school for additional information.

The Role of the Middle School Counselor

Because of the exciting changes that occur during the middle school years, there are many different reasons you may wish to talk with your school counselor.

One reason may be in the area of academics: the classes you're taking. Your school counselor wants to be sure you are learning as much as you can in each of your classes.

Another subject that middle school counselors talk to students about is friendships. Friendships may change in the middle school years. Sometimes it is very exciting because there are so many new friends to make. Sometimes it is confusing because old friendships change.

School counselors are available to discuss emotions: the way you feel inside. Sometimes things happen in your life that you have no control over, such as parents getting a divorce or a grandparent dying. When things like this happen, it hurts and you may need to talk to someone about the hurt.

The school counselor in your middle school wants to help you work through anything that you may have questions or concerns about. If you have a concern, come talk...we are here to help you.

This message has been brought to you by your school counselor. Contact the counselor in your school for additional information.

*Giveaway materials
for students*

Common Causes
of Teen Stress

- Taking tests
- Popularity
- Peer pressure
- Drugs and alcohol
- Dating and sex
- Problems at home
- Problems at school
- Competition
- Expectations

Warning Signs of Stress

- Restless sleep
- Fatigue
- Chronic headache or stomachache
- Changes in appetite
- Irritability or anger
- Discouragement and depression
- Withdrawal
- Avoidance
- Lack of concentration
- Drop in grades or work performance
- Nightmares

These "stress lists" can be printed up on separate cards or on the back of your business card.

Other examples of "positive lists" that can be provided to student stakeholders include:

Study Strategies

- Keep an assignment book
- If possible, study at the same time every day
- Study in a quiet place
- Do more difficult assignments first
- Start long-term assignments early; do them in phases

Compliments of your school counselor

Time-Management Strategies

- Be well organized
- Set priorities
- Establish objectives
- Focus on the objectives
- Make a daily "To Do" list
- Handle paper only once
- Don't procrastinate
- Do it right the first time
- Start to work immediately upon arrival at work or school
- Do hardest projects first
- Set realistic timelines
- Don't overextend; limit activities.

Compliments of your school counselor

Test-Preparation Strategies

- Plan ahead
- Study class notes
- Review textbook materials
- Ask questions about unclear information
- Anticipate possible test questions

Compliments of your school counselor

Test-Taking Strategies

- Relax!
- Glance over the test when you get it; budget your time.
- Look for clues to the answers.
- Do easier questions first; return to the difficult ones.
- Check your answers.

Compliments of your school counselor

Other ideas for working with students

Good News Gram...

Congratulations!
You made the Honor Roll for

_____

the _____ grading period!

Your school counselor

*You are invited
to bring your lunch
and spend your
lunchtime with
the school counselor*

Date:_____

Time:_____

Place:_____

Practical Examples of Materials to Use with Stakeholder Groups: Staff

Print the following on cards as giveaways, or on the reverse side of business cards

Administrator's Stress Reliever

The five-step, 10-second fix
When you feel stressed, irritated or anxious:
1. Smile as you think, "My body doesn't need this."
2. Close your eyes, picture yourself in a place you enjoy and breath deeply three times.
3. As you breathe out think, "I am calm."
4. Open your eyes as you think, "I can handle this."
5. Now approach or attack the task or problem.

This is a good technique to use before answering the phone, dealing with a difficult student, parent or teacher. Anyone can wait 10 seconds.

Note: If all else fails, make an appointment to see your favorite school counselor.

Tips for Dealing with Aggression

Do:
- Listen
- Write down what they say
- When they slow down, ask them what else is bothering them
- Exhaust their list of complaints
- Ask them to clarify any specific complaints that are too general
- Show them the list and ask if it is complete
- Ask them for suggestions for solving any of the problems that they've listed
- Write down the suggestions
- As much as possible, mirror their body posture during this process
- As they speak louder, you speak softer

Don't
- Argue
- Defend or become defensive
- Promise things you can't produce
- Own problems that belong to others
- Raise your voice
- Belittle or minimize the problem

Practical Examples of Materials to Use with Stakeholder Groups: Parents

Print the following on cards as giveaways, or on the reverse side of business cards

Questions About Stress: Strategies for Parents

What is stress?
Stress is the body's natural response to a demand. Everybody has stress. When a person is "stressed" or "under pressure," he/she is experiencing too much stress.

What effect does stress have?
Stress affects the way people think, feel and behave. An individual under stress can become angry, sad, fearful, or behave in a way inappropriate to the situation.

Is stress normal?
Everyone experiences stress because big and small demands are made on us all the time.

When does stress become a serious problem?
Stress is a serious problem when it gets in the way of success in school or work and makes it harder to enjoy relationships and leisure time. Stress that causes strong feelings or anger, anxiety, depression, or lack of control is serious stress.

Helping with Homework: Strategies for Parents

- Review assignments; develop a plan of action
- Divide the homework into segments; set time limits for each segment
- Provide a quiet study space
- Set a regular "homework time"
- Take short beaks between segments
- Help with homework; answer questions; give explanations. Don't do the homework!
- Check or review the homework with your child
- Contact the teacher with questions or problems

Talking to Your Child About Stress: Strategies for Parents

- Be a good listener
- Accept your child's feelings
- Don't dismiss or minimize your child's experiences
- Don't be judgmental
- Share your own similar experiences
- Help your child identify alternatives and consequences
- Let your child make his/her own decisions

Some bookmarks to share with parents

LET'S TALK ABOUT...

Parent-Teacher Conferences

It is imperative that you stay informed of your child's academic, social and emotional progress throughout his or her school years. Many parents have a tendency to become less active in their child's education as the child grows older. Unfortunately, that may be when your child needs you most.

Although reasons for conferences may vary, the primary goal is to exchange information. No one knows your child as well as you do. Your insights may prove to be invaluable.

Following are some tips that may help you prepare for your child's next conference:

1. Be on time. If you are unable to attend, or find you may be late, call the school.
2. Come prepared to give as well as receive information.
3. Ask specific questions regarding your child's progress in all areas.
4. If necessary, write your questions prior to the conference.
5. Ask whether it would be beneficial for your child to attend the conference.
6. Allowing your child to play an active role may help him/her accept responsibility for his/her own success

After all areas of concern are addressed, form an action plan.

This message has been brought to you by your school counselor. Contact the counselor in your child's school for additional information.

LET'S TALK ABOUT...

Your Child's Report Card

Your child's report card is a record of his or her accomplishments or lack of accomplishments. A time should be set aside to sit down and discuss the results in private. Ask questions about grades, classes, and activities. Try to avoid anger, criticism, blaming, comparisons, and too much praise. Focus on the positives first; point out achievements. As you discuss where your child needs to improve, offer support and encouragement.

Use the report card as a tool to set academic goals — goals that are challenging but reachable. Have your child list the things he or she is going to do to accomplish these goals. Do not focus on perfection and do not encourage competition against others. Evaluate the activities in which your child is involved; then assist your child in finding a healthy balance between schoolwork and activities by establishing a homework routine, providing special help, and supporting the school. Your attitude and actions as a parent can make a difference.

This message has been brought to you by your school counselor. Contact the counselor in your child's school for additional information.

LET'S TALK ABOUT...

Nobody Likes Me

"Nobody likes me." Is there a parent alive who hasn't heard this remark? As parents, sometimes we feel helpless in helping our child deal with relationships. So what do we do? Often all our children need is a sympathetic ear, a chance to vent and an opportunity to work through their pain verbally with us. They don't need to have a perfect solution. Often there is not a solution you can give them. Children need to be reassured. Take them seriously. Don't tell them that soon they'll get over it. You can help them put the problem in perspective. Believing in their ability to solve problems with your support can be a big first step. Ask them how they talk to their friends. Are there misunderstandings? Don't try to find a quick solution. Instead tell them that you will listen and help them problem-solve. Help them to know that a good place to begin building friendships is by being a good listener for others.

This message has been brought to you by your school counselor. Contact the counselor in your child's school for additional information.

Some bookmarks to share with parents

LET'S TALK ABOUT...

Building Self-Confidence

Children begin to build self-confidence through success and sometimes trial and error. In the developmental years children attempt to learn through accomplishing. Parenting becomes the fine art of supervising while allowing children to attempt jobs and begin to be more responsible. When parents support and encourage rather than perform a task themselves, they allow their children to develop decision-making skills. Self-esteem and self-confidence are nurtured throughout the life span as we learn and develop by accomplishing new tasks. Making decisions and incurring the consequences, whether they be negative or positive are sometimes the best learning situations.

Our children must learn to make decisions and know that they have gained through their own merits. They can then be more independent and self-confident.

This message has been brought to you by your school counselor. Contact the counselor in your child's school for additional information.

LET'S TALK ABOUT...

Building Self-Esteem – Part 1

As parents we want our children to like themselves. Children with self-esteem accept themselves, their strengths and weaknesses. They are often the children that other children look up to. A child with low self-esteem may lack self-confidence or be too willing to let others make decisions for them.

As a parent, you can develop self-esteem in your children by helping them feel competent and capable. Help them learn new skills. Let them know you believe in their competency. If you watch them in an athletic event, let them know you saw the things they did well. If they are doing household chores, praise the good things and teach the things that need to be improved. You might keep a scrapbook of accomplishments. Let your children do things for others. As your children grow older, give them more responsibilities — and more freedom. Periodically, rethink the rules you have set. It is very important to accept your child for who he/she is. Studies have shown that teenagers whose parents had been warm and accepting of them when they were younger had higher self-esteem.

This message has been brought to you by your school counselor. Contact the counselor in your child's school for additional information.

LET'S TALK ABOUT...

Divorce – Part I

Divorce is an issue that affects everyone in the family. More than one million marriages will end in divorce each year. Helping your child cope with divorce can be a challenging but rewarding task.

Communicating with your child is essential during this difficult time. The attitudes that parents maintain during the divorce can make a tremendous difference in how the child deals with the divorce.

Children of divorced parents have made the following suggestions:

1. Don't blame my other parent
2. Don't put me in the middle
3. Don't "bad-mouth" my other parent
4. Do let me talk to you about how I feel
5. Do answer my questions honestly
6. Do love me like you always have

Parents should not be afraid to seek help. Many schools offer support groups for children of divorce.

This message has been brought to you by your school counselor. Contact the counselor in your child's school for additional information.

*Some bookmarks to
share with parents*

LET'S TALK ABOUT...

Divorce – Part 2

Divorce has become more and more common in our society. It is normal for separating people to feel depression, anger, helplessness, loneliness and guilt. Your child may experience all of these same emotions and more. Most children eventually adjust, but current research tells us that the adjustment period can be as long as 5 to 10 years. Time and patience are the keys. Here are some suggestions that may help. If you and your child aren't ready to talk together, encourage him or her to find a trusted adult such as a school counselor or a family member who will listen and understand. It's very hard not to make your child take sides or feel that he or she is caught in the middle. If there are questions about whom the child will live with, let the child know it is not a matter of loving one parent more than the other. Don't be afraid to ask for help for you or your child.

This message has been brought to you by your school counselor. Contact the counselor in your child's school for additional information.

LET'S TALK ABOUT...

Heroes

Ralph Waldo Emerson once said, "The hero is no braver than the ordinary man, but he is brave five minutes longer."

Discussing heroes with our children enables us to share respect and admiration with them for people who show acts of courage, develop exceptional ability or model great strength of character. They help inspire us to become all we can be, and to recognize and appreciate the great thinkers and leaders of the world of tomorrow. Take time to discuss with your children the heroes in your family, community, nation and world.

The following are good questions to help in your discussion: Who has been a hero in your life and why? When have you been heroic for someone else or yourself? What do you feel are important qualities for a great leader to have? In what ways would you like to make a difference when you grow up?

This message has been brought to you by your school counselor. Contact the counselor in your child's school for additional information.

National School Counseling Week: Public Service Announcements

Sample PSA Scripts

PSA — Day One

On behalf of National School Counseling Week, we would like to recognize the theme "School Counselors: Exploring Human Potential." On Monday, schools take a long look at how students can explore their own potential. Remember, students, plan on success — but don't be afraid to fail. Although you probably don't remember, you've failed many times and learned a great deal each time. You fell the first time you tried to walk, but you got back up. Did you hit the ball the first time you were at bat? Babe Ruth struck out 1,330 times, but he also hit 714 homeruns! Don't worry about the opportunities that escape you, rather, be concerned about the opportunities you miss if you fail to try. On this first day of National School Counseling Week, students are encouraged to try something different and new, and to truly explore their potential!

PSA — Day Two

This is day two of National School Counseling Week, with its theme "School Counselors: Exploring Human Potential." Tuesday's special emphasis is on parents as navigators. Parents can assist their children in discovering their potential in many ways. Your interest in schoolwork, participation in school activities, your praise and encouragement for accomplishments, and your commitment to the concept of life-long learning are some of the ways your role as navigator takes on daily responsibility. The important thing to remember is that all children are special in their own way and the course they decide to follow is very much influenced by the guiding direction of loving parents. School counselors want parents to know that their interest and direction is valued and appreciated.

PSA — Day Three

This is day three of National School Counseling Week, with its theme "School Counselors: Exploring Human Potential." Today, we focus on "educators setting a course." As teachers steer and guide their students through various courses, they must recognize the different ability levels and learning styles with which they are working. Teachers can challenge their students to aim high and set goals for themselves. Through such actions as personal journals, linking subjects to careers, and showing genuine interest in student progress, teachers can help lead students toward appropriate educational and career choices. Remember, students, to call on teachers to assist you in charting your course for the future.

Sample PSA Scripts, cont.

PSA — Day Four

This is day four of National School Counseling Week, recognizing "School Counselors: Exploring Human Potential." Today, the focus is on areas outside the school as we take a look at potential discoveries in the community. Factory workers, bankers, artists, people in health professions, lawyers, farmers — to mention a few — all can play a significant part in helping young people discover their potential. As role models, community workers are often called upon to come to schools to talk about their careers. Students need "real-world" opportunities and experiences to prepare them for the future. There is much to be proud of in our communities and it is hoped many of these community members will take the opportunity to share some of their experiences and talents with school counseling programs.

PSA — Day Five

This is day five of National School Counseling Week, and this last day is devoted to discovering America's counselors. School counselors wear many hats throughout the year. Counselors are at varying times a child's teacher, counselor and friend. Counselors might help children discover their potential through involving them in self-esteem groups, researching careers, participating in school activities, or by consulting with teachers and parents. Students and parents are encouraged to meet with the school counselor and discuss personal concerns or issues, career planning or the goals of the school counseling program, or to just become acquainted. Take time to discover your school counselors, who they are and what they have to offer.

Sample PSA Scripts

PSA Sample

"I have no idea what classes John should take next year." "I don't see how we can possibly afford to send Jim to college." "Since our divorce, Steve's grades have dropped." "Jenny doesn't seek out friends and is alone most of the time."

Parents, do any of these sound like something you have heard yourself saying? If so, your school counselor could be the person to help you work through these fears.

Sponsored by the American School Counselor Association, National School Counseling Week is a good time to take advantage of the services your school counselor can perform for you. School counselors are trained professionals who can give you and your child advice about career planning and training, answer questions about achievement and discover barriers to learning, and help you and your child better communicate.

PSA Sample

"Chris is absent from class too much." "Debbie can't seem to get along with the other students." "Rick's behavior is erratic and his grades have dropped during the last few months."

If you're a teacher, these are concerns you face every day. School counselors work cooperatively with teachers to overcome problems that interfere with the learning process. Mutual awareness of what is happening in a student's life is an important factor in working with that student. This gives him or her at least two people concerned about him/her as a student and as a person. National School Counseling Week is a good time to reaffirm the cooperation necessary to deal with students and their problems.

Sample PSA Scripts

PSA Sample

Parents, have you caught yourself thinking any of the following, "My child's dress and friends have so drastically changed, I wonder what is going on?" "Since the divorce, Julie has become so withdrawn, her grades have dropped." "John keeps asking me which classes would best prepare him for college and an engineering degree — and I'm not sure what to tell him."

There are many challenges and dilemmas you face as your children grow up. Your school counselor is a good resource to help you and your child work through these questions. School counselors are trained professionals who can give you and your child advice about school achievement, interpersonal problems, and college or career planning. National School Counseling Week is a good time to call your child's counselor to learn about the counseling program and to take advantage of the services offered. Call your school counselor today.

National School Counseling Week: News Releases

Sample News Release

NEWS RELEASE

American School Counselor Association: National School Counseling Week

The celebration of National School Counseling Week, sponsored by the American School Counselor Association, during the week of February _____ through February _____ was announced today by _____, of the _____ school district.

National School Counseling Week emphasizes the value and importance of the role of the counselor in the school as the leading school professional who facilitates and supports the educational program and development of our nation's most precious resource, America's children. School counselors throughout the nation will be celebrating their contributions to their schools, communities, and states under this year's national theme:

_____

During this commemorative week, school counselors throughout America will be emphasizing how school counselors assist students to explore their worlds with the opportunities available to each of them for discovering their potentials; to expand their horizons of knowledge of themselves and their environments; and to learn how to apply this knowledge and potential to emerge in the 21st Century as holistic and healthy young adults.

Education today not only provides skill development in reading, writing and arithmetic, and the practical and fine arts, but the curriculum also includes instruction and counseling for the exploration and development of personal self-awareness and individual human potential.

To help celebrate National School Counseling Week, contact your local school and make an appointment to interview the school counselor. Arrange to visit one of your local schools and observe the ongoing programs that school counselors provide. Contact your local supervisor of counseling programs for further information. Counseling programs operate most effectively with the involvement, encouragement and participation of all members of the community. Help your school counseling program grow by exploring the personal contributions you can offer. Assist your school counselor by expanding the school's resources with the contribution of your expertise. Become a school counselor advocate and support the role of the counselor. Emerge together as a healthier community and nation in the 21st Century.

Sample News Release

Your Name:
Home Phone:
Office Phone:
Date:
Release Date:

Educational excellence is an expression often repeated but perhaps not understood. An appropriate definition of educational excellence is "helping each child achieve his or her full potential." In a world where children have more choices, family structures are more diverse, schools are under fire, economies are shifting, and communities feel the stress of change from all segments of society, helping children achieve their potential is a monumental task.

The first week of February is National School Counseling Week, sponsored by the American School Counselor Association. The theme of this annual observance is
_____. The purpose is to focus on school counselors with their special skills in promoting educational, social and personal growth in students. School counseling programs have been developed and improved to meet the challenge of assisting youth with living successfully in today's complex society.

Students, parents, counselors, teachers, administrators, businesspeople and the community are all important components that share responsibility in the effort to achieve educational excellence. School counselors are often the important liaison or "vital link" which enables all these groups to work together. Trained school counselors are important professionals who are proud of their role in making a positive difference in the lives of the students they serve.

Note: You may wish to personalize this news release by giving details of your celebration activities and the names of the school counselors in your district.

Contact:
Phone:
Address:

School Counselors Provide a Vision of Hope

National School Counseling Week, sponsored by the American School Counselor Association, is scheduled for February [insert dates]. National School Counseling Week is the time to focus public attention on the unique contribution of professional school counselors. Using the theme, A Vision of Hope, National School Counseling Week highlights the tremendous impact that counselors can have in helping students achieve school success.

School counselors are certified, experienced educators with a master's degree in guidance and counseling. The combination of their training and experience makes them an integral part of the total educational program by assisting students, teachers, parents, and administrators. Every day, school counselors and school counseling programs work to address the personal/social, academic and career needs of all students. Their ultimate goal is to enable all students to achieve success in school and to become responsible and productive members of our society.

More than 14,000 school counselors nationwide will be participating in the week's festivities. Many school counselors will be hosting special events and activities in order to call attention to their specific contributions to the educational process. If you have questions or concerns, please contact your child's school counselor. They are there to help. School counselors make a difference every day in the lives of children

Adapted with permission from The Ohio School Counselor Association.

Sample Newsletter Article for
National School Counselor's Week

"Counselors' Corner"

National School Counseling Week is scheduled for February [insert dates]. National School Counseling Week allows us to celebrate the contributions that we as school counselors make for the students in our school. It also gives us the chance to thank those who work with us. We would like to thank the other educators with whom we work for their support and cooperation. We would also like to thank the PTSA for the many projects they support in our school. Finally, we would like to thank all the parents who entrust us with their sons and daughters. We greatly appreciate your kind works and support of our efforts.

National School Counseling Week affords us the opportunity to share our role and vision. We see ourselves as a vital part of the educational program by assisting students, teachers, parents, and administrators. We have training and experience in both counseling and teaching. In Ohio, most counselors are certified, experienced teachers with a master's degree in school guidance and counseling. The combination of our training and teaching experience allows us to effectively work with students, parents, and teachers.

We work to assist in the personal, social, academic and career growth of our students. We achieve this in many different ways. Sometimes this could mean helping students and/or families work through personal concerns that distract the students from school. At other times, we may serve as an organizational or study-skill coach. Our ultimate goal is to help our students achieve success in school and to become responsible and productive members of our society.

If you have concerns, or if we can be of assistance to you in any way, please contact the school office to make an appointment or to speak to one of us.

Adapted with permission from The Ohio School Counselor Association.

PROCLAMATION

National School Counseling Week

WHEREAS, school counselors are employed in public and private schools to help students reach their full potential; and

WHEREAS, school counselors are actively committed to helping students explore their abilities, strengths, interests, and talents as these traits relate to career awareness and development; and

WHEREAS, school counselors help parents focus on ways to further the educational, personal and social growth of their children; and

WHEREAS, school counselors work with teachers and other educators to help students explore their potential and set realistic goals for themselves; and

WHEREAS, school counselors seek to identify and utilize community resources that can enhance and complement comprehensive school counseling programs and help students become productive members of society; and

WHEREAS, comprehensive developmental school counseling programs are considered an integral part of the educational process that enables all students to achieve success in school;

Therefore, I, _____ do hereby proclaim February _____, as National School Counseling Week.

National School Counseling Week

National School Counseling Week, sponsored by the American School Counseling Association, is scheduled for February [insert dates]. During the week the guidance department will be focusing public attention on the unique contributions of its counselors.

The counselors will be hosting special events and implementing special activities to call attention to their significant contributions to the educational process.

Monday

We focus on partnerships with our support staff and honor our secretaries, clerks, bus drivers, cafeteria staff, and maintenance workers.

Tuesday

We recognize the contributions of the junior high homeroom representatives with a breakfast.

Wednesday

We recognize the contributions of the high school class officers with a luncheon.

Thursday

We thank the administration, the school council, and the school committee.

Friday

We celebrate our teachers, and thank them for their dedication and commitment to our students.

The "Teacher of the Year" will be announced.

Adapted with permission from Triton Guidance, Massachusetts.

Why Elementary School Counselors?

The Challenge:

According to "Every Day in America, 1996," published by the Children's Defense Fund:

Every day in the United States:

- Three children and youths under 25 die from HIV infection.
- Six children and youths under 20 commit suicide.
- 13 children and youths are homicide victims.
- 16 children and youths are killed by firearms.
- 316 children under 18 are arrested for violent crimes.
- 1,420 babies are born to teen mothers.
- 2,556 babies are born into poverty.
- 3,356 students drop out each school day.
- 5,702 children under 18 are arrested.
- 13,076 public school students are suspended each school day.

For many people, the word "counselor" takes them back to the image of someone they saw a few times in high school to help them with their class schedules, testing, college applications and discipline. Elementary counselors are responding to today's needs by providing children with comprehensive and developmental school counseling programs.

A Certified and/or Licensed Professional:

All professional school counselors must have a master's degree and meet other certification requirements as defined by each state.

The Developmental Needs of Elementary School Students

Elementary school is a time when students develop attitudes concerning school, self, peers, social groups and family. It is a time when students develop decision-making, communication and life-training skills and character values. Comprehensive developmental counseling is based on prevention, providing goals which are integrated into all aspects of children's lives. Early identification and intervention of children's problems are essential to change some of the current statistics regarding self-destructive behaviors. If we wait until children are in middle or high school to address these problems, we lose the opportunity to help them achieve their potential, as well as feelings of dignity and self-worth. For many children, the school counselor may be the one person who provides an atmosphere of safety, trust and positive regard.

Elementary School Counselors:

- implement effective classroom guidance focusing on: understanding self and others; coping strategies; peer relationships and effective social skills; communication, problem-solving, decision-making, conflict resolution, and study skills; career awareness and the world of work; substance education; multicultural awareness.
- Provide individual and small group counseling dealing with: self-image and self-esteem; personal adjustment; family issues; interpersonal concerns; academic development; behavior modification; as well as peer facilitation and peer mediation.
- Provide assessment by helping students identify their skills, abilities, achievements and interests through counseling and guidance activities and interpretation of standardized tests.
- Work with specialized populations and needs that require special attention, such as culturally diverse populations and students of varying abilities.
- Develop students' career awareness as a lifelong process of forming basic values, attitudes and interests regarding their future world of work.
- Coordinate school, community and business resources; schoolwide guidance-related activities; and extracurricular programs which promote students' personal growth and skill development.
- Provide consultation with teachers, administrators, school psychologists, school social workers, and outside agencies and social services concerning the welfare of the students.
- Make appropriate referrals for special services for students and families within the school and community.
- Communicate and exchange information with parents/guardians by way of conferences, parent education workshops and newsletters.
- Participate as members of the school improvement and interdisciplinary teams and work as liaisons with PTA.

Why Elementary School Counselors?

Elementary school years set the tone for developing the skills, knowledge and attitudes necessary for our children to become healthy, productive adults. With a comprehensive developmental counseling program, counselors work as a team with school parents and community to create a caring atmosphere whereby children's needs are met through prevention, early identification and intervention.

Adopted by the ASCA Governing Board, April 1997.

Why Middle School Counselors?

The Challenge:

According to "Every Day in America, 1996," published by the Children's Defense Fund:

Every day in the United States:

- Three children and youths under 25 die from HIV infection.
- Six children and youths under 20 commit suicide.
- 13 children and youths are homicide victims.
- 16 children and youths are killed by firearms.
- 316 children under 18 are arrested for violent crimes.
- 1,420 babies are born to teen mothers.
- 2,556 babies are born into poverty.
- 3,356 students drop out each school day.
- 5,702 children under 18 are arrested.
- 13,076 public school students are suspended each school day.

School Counselors Have Changed:

Caring, professional school counselors are responding to the needs of today's youth through comprehensive school counseling programs.

A Certified and/or Licensed Professional:

All professional school counselors must have a master's degree and meet other certification requirements as defined by each state. Most have previous teaching experience. Professional middle school counselors have training and experience in understanding the developmental tasks of 11 to 15 year olds and are competent in counseling, consulting and coordinating.

The Developmental Needs of Middle School Students

Middle school is an exciting but frustrating time for students in addition to their parents and teachers. Transition is the key word. Through middle school years, physical and psychological changes abound. During their journey from childhood to adolescence, students are characterized by:

- Being very active, yet easily fatigued due to rapid physical growth
- Searching for their own unique identity, turning more toward their peers rather than to their parents for ideas and affirmation
- Being extremely sensitive to comments from others
- Relying heavily on friends to provide comfort, understanding and approval

A Comprehensive and Developmental Program

Internal changes, coupled with the challenges of the outside world, reinforce the goal of middle school counselors: to teach students skills to help them through this difficult stage of life and to use these skills on a daily basis. To accomplish this, middle school counselors provide and carry out a comprehensive counseling program that focuses on the uniqueness of students in three areas of development – academic, career and personal/social. Designed for all students, student competencies provide goals that are integrated throughout the entire school curriculum and environment. These goals are the engine that drives the program components including the guidance curriculum, individual planning, counseling and program management.

School Counselors Work With Many People in a Variety of Ways

Keeping the developmental program goals in mind, middle school counselors work with students in groups and individually, depending on the nature of the problem, issue or topic. They provide transition activities between elementary and middle school and middle and high school. Middle school counselors support advisory programs by participating in the development and implementation of activities and offering in-services to teachers and administrators.

Working with teachers and administrators, middle school counselors participate as members of school improvement and interdisciplinary teams. They serve as consultants to teachers and parents by providing information regarding meeting student academic and emotional needs. Working together, teachers, administrators and middle school counselors build a program that is based on characteristics of middle school students, the connectedness of school and home life and the importance of peer and adult relationships.

In the community, the school counselor serves as a coordinator and manager of indirect services that assist students. They are a liaison between school educational agencies and social services, and they collaborate with business and industry to provide meaningful career exploration opportunities for all students.

Parent partnerships are equally important to the success of a middle school counseling program. Parents serve on advisory committees, help evaluate the current program and give input for changes within the program. Finally, middle school counselors assist parents in looking at the "whole" child, including education, career and personal/social perspectives.

The middle school counselor also works extensively with the administration. Through collaboration, a student-centered environment that emphasizes developmental guidance can be developed, creating a climate that enhances self-esteem, student growth and academic achievement.

Why Middle School Counselors?

Middle school years can be positive ones of self-discovery for children. Together, professional middle school counselors, parents, teachers, administrators and community members can help students focus on the journey of transition through a collaborative effort using a comprehensive developmental counseling program, patience, understanding and, above all, caring.

Adopted by the ASCA Governing Board, April 1997.

Why High School Counselors?

The Challenge:

In our changing world:

- By age 21, today's young people have faced more decisions than their grandparents faced in a lifetime.
- One out of five families moves each year.
- Everyone faces career decisions.
- Young people face greater risks than previous generations.
- Young people face critical decisions about sexuality.
- Young people face increasing violence in our society and in their schools.
- Some young people face hopelessness that can lead to self-destructive behaviors.

A Certified and/or Licensed Professional

Counselor qualifications include certification defined by each state after achieving specific competencies including endorsement from a state-approved master's degree program of preparation.

The Developmental Needs of High School Students

High school is a time of decisions. Students are deciding who they are, where they fit, what they are good at and how to move forward. Socialization is the key word. During this time in high school, students are characterized by:

- Searching and evaluating their strengths, skills and abilities.
- Tuning into peer acceptance and feedback.
- Separating from parents/family to explore and define their independence.
- Planning for the future.

A Comprehensive and Developmental Program

Services provided for students are connected to a comprehensive counseling model that focuses on the needs of the students in three areas of development:
academic, career and personal/social. These areas are inter-related and cannot be addressed in isolation. Comprehensive, developmental counseling services are designed for all students.

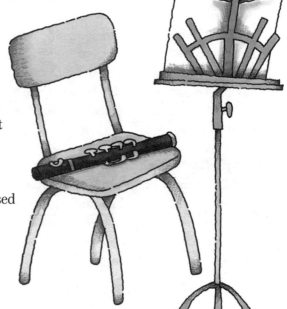

High School Counselors Believe

- Young people have dignity and worth as human beings.
- Young people need to experience significance in their school and community.
- Young people have the ability to succeed and become contributing members of our society.
- Young people need guidance and support from school, parents and community as they seek to find their place in society.
- Schools, parents and communities that communicate and collaborate provide the most effective support to young people.

High School Counselors

- Provide direct counseling services to students individually and in support groups.
- Provide education and support services to parents.
- Provide consultation services to teachers.
- Provide staff inservice.
- Facilitate referrals to community support services.
- Advise students on academic planning.
- Provide career guidance to students.
- Provide career information to parents.
- Maintain an up-to-date library of career and post-secondary school information.
- Network with post-secondary schools.
- Serve on school and community committees addressing the needs of young people.

Why High School Counselors?

High school years are full of excitement, frustration, disappointment and hope. It is a time students begin to discover what the future holds for them. With a comprehensive developmental counseling program, students can receive accurate information, concrete experiences and successful planning to take the steps necessary to become a productive and contributing member of society. Together, professional school counselors, parents and the community can provide the most effective support for young people.

Adopted by the ASCA Governing Board, April 1997.

Why Post-secondary Counselors, Counselor Supervisors and Counselor Educators?

The Challenge

Increased needs of students, parents, teachers and other school personnel require that school counselors/supervisors and counselor educators continually expand their knowledge and skills. State certification requirements for school counselors in supervisory roles have increased for both initial certification and continuing education. In addition, national professional certification organizations require continuing in-service training and supervision.

A Certified and/or Licensed Professional

All counselors must hold a master's degree and meet additional certification requirements as defined by each state. These degree and certification requirements include the completion of supervised practicum and internship experiences. Many states require that school counselors/supervisors hold administrative and/or supervisory licenses in addition to school counseling certification.

The Professional Development Needs of School Counselor Supervisors, Post-secondary Counselors and Counselor Educators

The professional preparation and continuing education of school counselor supervisors, post-secondary counselors and counselor educators includes:

- Pre-service instruction and supervision in the development of counseling skills and school counseling program curricula
- Supervised field experiences and internships in public schools
- In-service seminars and workshops that enhance program implementation through individual and group supervision
- Appropriate state credentials
- Post-master's degree study and/or doctoral degree in school district administration, supervision, counselor education, counseling psychology or a related area.

Supervision of a Comprehensive and Developmental School Counseling Program

A comprehensive and developmental school counseling program focuses on the needs of all students in three areas of development: academic, career and personal/social. The primary responsibility of the school counselor supervisor in a school district is to design and implement a comprehensive, developmental counseling program based upon the identified needs of the students in the individual school building or system. The coordination and supervision of the school counseling program at college/university level ensures the quality of the program students receive throughout their K-12 educational training.

Counselor Supervisors and Counselor Educators also:

- Coordinate the implementation of school counseling services, K-12
- Provide individual and group supervision to school counselors in practice
- Collaborate in the supervision of school counseling interns
- Coordinate continuing education for school counselors
- Provide instruction to pre-service counselor education students in the development of counseling skills and counseling program curricula
- Provide individual and group supervision to pre-service counselor education students

Why Counselor Supervisors/Educators?

The development and implementation of comprehensive school counseling programs requires a collaborative effort among well-trained, highly competent professional school counselors. Counselor supervisors and educators provide in-service and pre-service instruction and supervision to promote the development and enhancement of school counselor training and professional development. This ensures that school counselors deliver school counseling programs in a comprehensive and systematic manner to all students.

Accountability/Summary

Employment setting probably determines accountability. Examples: School counseling supervisions generally report to district-level administrators, superintendent and school boards. A counseling supervisor for a student being supervised for licensure would be governed by that body's code of ethics and criteria for licensure. A post-secondary counselor would be supervised or governed by the hierarchy within its employing body.

In summary, counselors in the post-secondary/supervisor category must be viewed in their total employment environment when considering credentialing requirements, program delivery and context, co-workers and job associates and evaluation/accountability standards.

Adopted by the ASCA Governing Board, April 1997.

School Counselors

Assist students in career planning and decision-making in:

- Developing skills in career decision-making

- Analyzing the inter-relationships of interest and abilities

- Understanding career stereotypes

- Exploring careers through shadowing experiences

- Utilizing the career planning-process

Adapted with permission from the Colorado School Counselor Association

School Counselors

Assist students in educational planning in:

- Setting and reaching academic goals

- Developing a positive attitude toward learning

- Developing an education plan

- Understanding individual learning styles

- Improving test-taking skills

- Recognizing and utilizing academic strengths

Adapted with permission from the Colorado School Counselor Association

School Counselors

Help students grow personally and socially in:

- Developing self-knowledge

- Making effective decisions

- Developing relationship skills

- Learning healthy choices

- Improving responsibility

- Resolving conflicts

Adapted with permission from the Colorado School Counselor Association

School-to-Work Transition Curriculum Components

Self-Knowledge:

• School counselors assist students and help them learn about themselves and their individual strengths through a variety of tests, assessments and activities.

• School counselors work with students individually and in groups.

• School counselors help students develop communication and interpersonal skills needed in the workplace.

Adapted with permission from the Colorado School Counselor Association

Occupational and Educational Exploration

• School counselors help students investigate qualifications for various occupations and learn about requirements for further education and training.

• School counselors collaborate with teachers to incorporate career awareness and exploration activities into the classroom curriculum.

• School counselors arrange or provide opportunities for students experiential learning, mentoring, community service, internships, job shadowing, career seminars and peer teaching.

• School counselors support and coordinate the collaborative effort of administrators, teachers, parents and business and industry representatives.

Adapted with permission from the Colorado School Counselor Association

Career Planning

- School counselors help students use information gained through self-knowledge and occupational and educational exploration to develop and revise plans to reach their career goals.

- School counselors provide student training in career decision-making and planning.

- School counselors coordinate the development of student career plans and portfolios collaborating with parents' and teachers and recognizing the important role parents play in their children's career planning and goal setting.

Adapted with permission from the ASCA and NCDA Joint Initiative

Components of a Comprehensive, Developmental School Counseling Program

Guidance Curriculum:

Consists of structured developmental experiences presented through classroom and group activities to K-post.

Purpose is to provide all students at all grade levels with knowledge and assistance in acquiring and using life skills.

Individual Planning:

Consists of planned and counselor-directed activities that help all students plan, monitor and manage their own learning as well as their personal and career development.

● Individual Appraisal: Counselors assist students in analyzing and evaluating students' abilities, interests, skills and achievement.

● Individual Advisement: Counselors assist students in establishing personal, social, educational and occupational goals, involving parents, students and school.

● Placement: Counselors assist students in making the transition from school to school, to work and/or additional post-secondary education training.

Responsive Services:

Consist of activities to meet the immediate needs and concerns of students.

● Consultation: Counselors consult with parents, teachers, other educators and community agencies regarding strategies to help students.

● Personal Counseling: Counseling is provided on a small-group or individual basis for students.

● Crisis Counseling: Counseling and support are provided to students and their families facing emergency situations.

● Referral: Counselors use referral sources to deal with crises such as suicide, violence, abuse and terminal illness.

System Support:

Consists of management activities that establish, maintain and enhance the total guidance program.

- Professional Development: Counselors are actively involved regularly in updating their professional knowledge and skills.

- Staff and Community Relations: Counselors orient staff and the community to the comprehensive, developmental, standards-based school counseling program.

- Consultation with Teachers: Counselors need to consult with teachers and other staff members to provide information, to support staff and to receive feedback on emerging needs of students.

- Advisory Councils: Counselors support other programs through service on departmental curriculum committees, community committees, etc.

- Community outreach: Counselors participate in activities designed to help counselors become knowledgeable about community resources and referral agencies.

- Program Management and Operations: Counselors coordinate planning and management tasks that support the activities of a comprehensive guidance and counseling program.

- Research and Development: Counselors engage in and provide for program evaluation, data analysis, follow-up studies and the continued development of updating learning activities and resources.

Adapted with permission from Dr. Normal Gysbers, Comprehensive Guidance Programs That Work

Advantages of Employing a School Counselor

School Counselors Are:

- Credentialed/licensed professional educators

- Experienced in developmental issues of school-aged children

- Trained to provide relevant, practical recommendations to administration, parents, teaching staff

- Knowledgeable about educational protocol

- Cost-effective as they provide early intervention and prevention ideas and strategies that help eliminate the need for more costly evaluations and placements

- Committed to their students, staff, parents and district to which they are employed

- Readily available to school personnel, students and families in times of crisis

- Able to provide a wide range of services not easily purchased via private contracts such as consultations with family, administration, teachers, classroom guidance programs, prevention programs, crisis-intervention programs, career counseling, in-service training, teaming

- Available for students and staff of the school system to provide support, consultation and intervention.

Adapted with permission from the Advocacy Task Force for School Psychologists

National School Counseling Week: Practical Ideas

Sample Practical Ideas

Secret Pal Program

I would like to organize a secret pal program to be run during National School Counseling Week. This is not a competition with extravagant gifts or a chance to spend a lot of money. It is an entirely voluntary opportunity to acknowledge a colleague, a co-worker, a friend...Each of the five days of NSCW, you will be asked to extend some recognition to your secret pal; it could be a note, an apple, a favorite snack, helping out with something you know they could use some support with, a compliment, a pat on the back. If you would like to participate, please circle "Yes" next to your name below. Names will be picked later this week, in advance of NSCW.

[attach your staff routing list here...]

This will add warmth to your winter!

Secret Pals will be picked on _____

Each day, for 5 days, please leave a small gift for your Secret Pal. The idea is not to be extravagant or to leave expensive gifts; more gifts of the heart; recognition and appreciation...On Friday, Secret Pals concludes, but we do not reveal as a lesson in giving. Thank you for your participation!

With love,

Thank you breakfast in the Teacher's Room in honor of National School Counseling Week

One possibility for a secret pal gift for your pal or for someone you think has a really fun class!

Laughter
and fun bubbles
from your classroom
and adds joy
to everyone
at Caldwell School!!

Thank you!!!

A card attached to a basket of fresh strawberries is a delicious and fun way to acknowledge your secret pal!

You're
Berry
special!

Practical
Ideas

Thank you teachers

As part of our celebration activities for National School Counseling week, we want to thank you, the teachers. The counseling department applauds your hard work and commitment to our students. We recognize that you are on the front line in dealing with the students. Each year the task of teaching has become more difficult. Increasing class size and meeting the needs of all students has put a special burden on our teachers. This note is to let you know that your diligent work is sincerely appreciated.

Used with permission from Triton Guidance, MA.

NATIONAL SCHOOL COUNSELING WEEK

Take a break on us!

We want you to know how much we appreciate all of your efforts. We especially want to thank you for all of the support you give to us throughout the year. So take a few minutes to take a break on us!

Teacher Tissues

When you find a box of tissues in a classroom, it is generally there for the purpose of providing mops for runny little noses. Only a teacher can realize the real necessity for having a supply of tissues in the classroom within reach of the teacher.

Tears are shed by teachers on many occasions and for many reasons. When a student is distraught after being dealt a hard blow in life, caring teachers shed tears of compassion as they help the young person struggle through. These tears can easily be tears of despair when a student chooses to follow a path in life that can only lead to trouble or failure.

Tears of grief are shed not only when a student loses his or her life, but also for the loss of a mind when a student gives up on obtaining an education or reaching his or her potential. The majority of tears shed by teachers are far more free flowing. They are the tears of joy when students achieve success whether this success is as simple as a kindergartener tying a shoe for the first time or as rewarding as watching a student realize his or her ultimate dreams in life.

We are providing you with this packet of tissues since we know the tears of a teacher are many and frequent. May they never run dry.

Used with Permission from Ohio School Counseling Association NSCW 2000 Packet

*Practical
Ideas*

The True Identity of a Lifesaver®

This simple roll of Lifesavers® is provided for you as a reminder of the ultimate purpose and goal of an educator: that of a lifesaver.

The five flavors represent five ways through which you can save or touch the lives of young people. The first is through your Leadership: the guidance you give and the example you set for students in your charge. The second is through the Lessons you teach and show by the knowledge you impart to your students that will serve them in the future. The third is by Listening: the friendly ear that you always have ready to hear what students need to express, whether it is positive or negative. The next is the Love you carry in your heart for your students and the sensitivity and understanding that springs from that love. The final way is through your Life; the life you dedicated to and the time you give to the education of children.

Each individual Lifesaver® represents a present or former student. As you munch your way through this roll of Lifesavers®, can you name a student whose life you have saved or touched because (and read these words with pride) YOU ARE A TEACHER?

Used with permission from Nancy Volmer, Teacher-Educator, Galion City Schools, Ohio SCA NSCW

It's a "treat" to work with you!
(Attach candy here)

Popcorn

Who doesn't love popcorn? Isn't one of the reasons we love it so much because we find it fascinating? Imagine that the kernels inside this bag are the students in our school.

You, whether you are a teacher, administrator, counselor, aide, bus driver, cook, or custodian, can be the fire that helps transform students into the fascinating individuals they could not have become without you. Kind words, actions and encouragement are all tools we have within our reach to stoke the fire.

Not all of the kernels develop at once. Some take a little more time and coaxing than others, but eventually, with the right conditions they blossom!

Keep the fire burning and never forget the anticipation and surprise of never knowing just when the kernels will pop!

*Bookmarks
to Share*

School Counselors

Are here to help with:
- Study skills
- Organization
- Personal conflict
- Conflict resolution
- Stress management
- Family concerns
- Scheduling
- Self-esteem
- Goal-setting
- Support during crises
- Career exploration
- New student support

*Let us know
how we can help You!*

**NATIONAL
SCHOOL
COUNSELING
WEEK**

*When you touch
the life of a child
you touch eternity.*

**NATIONAL
SCHOOL
COUNSELING
WEEK**

Relevant Quotes

You must be the change you
wish to see in the world.
—Ghandi

Use what talents you possess;
the woods would be very
silent if no birds sang except
those that sang best.
—Henry Van Dyke

They may forget what you
said, but they will never
forget how you made
them feel.
—Carl W. Buechner

Sample Handout

Benefits of school counseling programs

Comprehensive school guidance and counseling programs positively affect students, parents, teachers, administrators, boards and departments of education, school counselors, counselor educators, post-secondary institutions, student services personnel, business and industry, and the community. The benefits to each of these groups include the following:

Benefits for Students
1. Relates educational programs to future success.
2. Facilitates career exploration and development.
3. Develops decision-making and problem-solving skills.
4. Assists in acquiring knowledge of self and others.
5. Enhances personal development.
6. Assists in developing effective interpersonal relationship skills.
7. Broadens knowledge of a changing world.
8. Provides advocacy for students.
9. Encourages facilitative, cooperative peer interactions.
10. Fosters resiliency factors for students.
11. Ensures equitable access to educational opportunities.

Benefits for Parents
1. Provides support for parents in advocating for their child's academic, career, and personal/social development.
2. Develops a system for their child's long-range planning and learning.
3. Increases opportunities for parent/school interaction.
4. Enables parents to access school and community resources.

Benefits for Teachers
1. Provides an interdisciplinary team effort to address student needs and educational goals.
2. Provides skill development for teachers in classroom management, teaching effectiveness and affective education.
3. Provides consultation to assist teachers in their guidance role.

Benefits for Administrators
1. Integrates school counseling with the academic mission of the school.
2. Provides a program structure with specific content.
3. Assists administration to effectively use school counselors to enhance learning and development for all students.
4. Provides a means of evaluating school counseling programs.

Sample Handout

Benefits for Boards and Departments of Education
1. Provides a rationale for implementing a comprehensive developmental counseling program.
2. Provides assurance that a quality counseling program is available to all students.
3. Demonstrates the necessity of appropriate levels of funding for implementation.
4. Supports appropriate accreditation and staffing.
5. Provides a basis for determining funding allocations for school counseling programs.
6. Furnishes program information to the community.
7. Gives ongoing information about student competencies and standards for excellence attained through school counseling program efforts.

Benefits for School Counselors
1. Provides a clearly defined role and function.
2. Reduces non-counseling functions.
3. Provides direct service to all students.
4. Provides a tool for program management and accountability.
5. Enhances the role of the school counselor as a student advocate.
6. Ensures involvement in the academic mission of the school.

Benefits for Counselor Educators
1. Enhances collaboration between counselor education programs and public schools.
2. Provides exemplary supervision sites for school counseling internships.
3. Increases opportunities for collaborative research on school counseling program effectiveness.

Benefits for Post-secondary Institutions
1. Enhances articulation and transition of students to post-secondary institutions.
2. Prepares students for advanced educational opportunities.
3. Motivates students to seek a wide range of post-secondary options, including college.

Benefits for Student Services Personnel
1. Provides school psychologists, social workers, and other professional student services personnel with a clear definition of the school counselor's role.
2. Clarifies areas of overlapping responsibilities.
3. Fosters a positive team approach, enhancing cooperative working relationships.

Adapted with permission from: ASCA's "Sharing the Vision, National Standards for School Counseling Programs," Carol Dahir and Chari Campbell.